FASSOLIA PLAKI—cold bean stew (Armenian)   6 servings

CHI KUFTA—steak tartare...Armenian style   6 servings

PATLIJANOV DOLMA—Eggplant stuffed w/bulghour & lamb
(Armenian)   4–6 servings

1 lb chopped lamb   1/2 c tomato sauce
1/4 c large bulghour   12 baby eggplants
1 onion, chopped   1 1/2 c water
salt   juice of 1/2 lemon
1/8 tsp pepper

Combine lamb, bulghour, onion, 1 tsp salt, pepper, & half
of the tomato sauce. Mix w/hands. Wash the eggplants w/
cold water. Cut off the stem end, & w/an apple corer,
scoop out the pulp & leave only the thin purple shell.
Fill w/the meat mixture & arrange in saucepan. Combine
the water w/the bal. of the tomato sauce, the lemon
juice, & a little salt to taste, & pour the liquid into
the saucepan. Bring the liquid to a boil, & lower the
flame. Place a cover on the saucepan, & simmer 45 min.
Serve hot w/ madzoon=yoghurt

TURKISH COOKING

IRFAN ORGA

TURKISH
COOKING

ANDRE DEUTSCH

FIRST PUBLISHED 1958 BY
ANDRE DEUTSCH LIMITED
105 GREAT RUSSELL STREET
LONDON WCI
© IRFAN ORGA 1958
SECOND IMPRESSION OCTOBER 1963
THIRD IMPRESSION APRIL 1968
FOURTH IMPRESSION MAY 1971
FIFTH IMPRESSION FEBRUARY 1975
REPRINTED BY LITHOGRAPHY
BY EBENEZER BAYLIS AND SON LIMITED
THE TRINITY PRESS WORCESTER AND LONDON

ISBN 0 233 96340 5

CONTENTS

TABLE OF
APPROXIMATE MEASUREMENTS

Almonds (shelled)	1 lb	approx. 3½ cups
Bananas (sliced)	1 lb	2½ cups
Butter	1 lb	2 cups
Cheese (grated)	1 lb	4 cups
Cheese (soft white)	1 lb	2 cups
Cream (double) and milk	1 pint	2 cups
Cream (whipped)	1 pint	4 cups
Dates (whole)	1 lb	2¼ cups
Dates (stoned)	1 lb	2 cups
Figs (cut up)	1 lb	2¾ cups
Flour (sifted)	1 lb	4 cups
Raisins	1 lb	2¾ cups
Rice	1 lb	2¼ cups
Sugar (brown)	1 lb	2 cups
Sugar (caster)	1 lb	2¼ cups
Sugar (icing, sifted)	1 lb	3¼ cups
Walnuts (shelled)	1 lb	4 cups

IMPORTANT NOTE

All measurements in this book are calculated against the Pyrex Standard measuring cups (dry and liquid), assuming that 250 c.cs. equals 1 cup.

HERBS AND SPICES

The judicious use of herbs and spices is most important in the intelligent preparation of food, since well cooked dishes will be improved and dull dishes enriched with a subtle flavour. It has been said that the Turks use too much garlic in their food – as well as too much of almost every kind of herb – but this sort of accusation must always be suspect since all nations evolve their dishes to suit their own palate. Any of the recipes in this book can dispense with garlic but, in a Turk's opinion, much of the flavour will have been lost thereby so I would say to anyone who tries these recipes: leave at least an *aroma* of garlic floating around the dish!

Herbs should, if possible, be garden fresh, but if dried herbs are used they should be kept in a tightly covered *tin* (not a glass jar) and renewed the moment their first freshness has gone. I am giving a list of the most important herbs used in Turkish cookery and a few general ideas of how to use them.

Allspice (Baharat). Sparingly in some desserts, fish dishes and meats.

Anise (Anason). Use the young leaves in salads and the seeds for breads or white cheeses.

Basil (Feslegen). An excellent and distinctive herb for all salad dishes, white cheeses, beef, veal, fish and sauces. A corrective of rich, fatty dishes.

Bay Leaf (Defne Yapragi). The leaves should be used sparingly in soups, meats, fish and poultry dishes.

Caraway Seeds (Kimyon). The seeds give a delicious flavour when grilled with meats and are very good mixed with soft, white cheese.

Chervil (Baharat). One of the best of all salad herbs. Also good with egg dishes, soups, white cheese, poultry and fish.

Chives (Yaban Sarumsagi). Gives a subtle and delicate onion

7

flavour and is indispensable with new potatoes, omelettes and white cheese. Also good with fish and certain sauces.

Cinnamon (Tarcin). Excellent in cold dolma stuffing and with braised meats.

Coriander Seed (Cereotu). Delicate aroma and excellent in stews.

Dill (Tereotu). Good with lamb, fish, nearly all soups, salads and vegetable dishes served hot.

Fennel (Dereotu). To be used with fish.

Garlic (Sarumsag). A herb with a history of 5,000 years. Pungent and stimulating. Can be used in some meat dishes and cold vegetable dishes and with yoğurt.

Mace (Kavassyi). For soups and, sparingly, in stocks. Distinctive flavour.

Marjoram, Sweet (Amarak). For sauces, soups, salads, beef, lamb, fish, poultry.

Mint (Nane). Excellent with new peas and new potatoes, salad dressings and lamb and many soup dishes as garnish.

Oregano (Yabani Amarak). Excellent with lamb and for stuffings.

Nutmeg (Zencefil). Grated in soups and in some sauces and cakes.

Parsley (Maydanoz). Soups, fish, eggs, meat dishes.

Poppy Seed (Haşhaş Tohumu). Excellent with white cheeses, breads and stews.

Rosemary (Biberine). Gives subtlety and distinction to beef, lamb, veal, sauces and vegetables.

Saffron (Safron). Indispensable in some kofte dishes and with pilav.

Sage (Ada Çayi). Fresh sage is far more satisfactory than the dried variety. As the flavour is very evident the leaves should be used sparingly with white cheeses, some fish dishes, beans, duck, veal and poultry.

Savory, Summer (Baharat). Leaves and flowers give a distinctive flavour to poultry, beef, lamb, veal, salads and some pilav dishes.

Savory, Winter (Kiş Baharat). Has a very mild and delicate flavour and is excellent with fish.

Sorrel (Kuzu Kulaği). Delicious with certain vegetable dishes and salads.

Tarragon (Tarhun). The crumbled leaves should be used sparingly in salads, soups, fish, dressings, veal and poultry.

Thyme (Kekik). This popular herb enriches and glorifies all thick soups, sauces, white cheeses, beef, veal, poultry and fish and some salad dressings and is particularly good with grilled chops.

PREFACE

During the preparation of this book of recipes I came across some facts which I had not previously taken much note of.

In the first place it was borne in upon me how extravagant-seeming the Turks are with regard to the raw materials of cookery. Butter, eggs, cream, cheese, oil, the most succulent cuts of meat, the breasts of chicken or turkey are all used on a grand scale and in a country where the cost of living is high and wages low, this must seem all the more startling to more austerity-led communities. The fact, however, which emerges with most significance is the conservatism of the people. Certain dishes are regional and traditional – Aubergine Mousakka, Imam Bayildi, Baklava, Chicken Pilav etc, and if the Turkish housewife wants to make any of these dishes – whether for a family occasion or a special Bayram day – she will unhesitatingly use all the butter, cream, eggs and olive oil called for, never dreaming of substituting inferior ingredients. Imam Bayildi, for instance, in her reckoning, requires just so much olive oil, etc, and if the recipe is altered even the merest fraction, it is *not* the dish which caused the original Imam to faint! I once asked my sister's cook in Istanbul why she used nine small eggs in the Revani she was making instead of six large ones. She replied without hesitation that the recipe called for nine *small* eggs. When questioned further she grew dumb with the inability to answer but allowed finally that when the recipe was first evolved (it was one of the many which came out of the Dolmabahçe Saray when the last Sultan was deposed) the nine small eggs were found to be more satisfactory than the six large ones! Further than that she would not go and she afterwards complained to my sister that I had become very 'Europeanised'. This fetish of tradition is a part of Turkey and Turkish cooking and some of the dishes are so old that nobody ever questions their make-up.

The craze for vitaminising food, for balancing meals so

11

that the greatest dietetic value may be extracted, is lost on the Turks; for centuries they have served well balanced meals quite by accident. Experts on vegetable dishes for generations – it must be remembered that the Turks, an Oriental people, were familiar with the cultivation of vegetables long before Pizarro swept down on Peru and brought back knowledge of the potato – they unknowingly vitaminised themselves by simply serving their vegetables in the liquor in which they were cooked.

Turks have always eaten better than any other people in the Eastern Mediterranean and quite early in Ottoman times they spread their cooking throughout the region as, later, the French were to spread their cooking throughout Europe. This is not to say that French influence has not penetrated as far as Turkey; it has indeed, but mostly to Istanbul or Ankara and none of these dishes are sacred to the Turks – they have no great weight of tradition attached to them, no stories with which to regale guests, no nostalgic memories of the great days. An agricultural people, dour, emotional and with little sense of humour, conservative by nature rather than circumstances, the Turks have, since the Eleventh Century, been very much to the forefront in the affairs of the Middle East.

The Eleventh and Twelfth Centuries were, undoubtedly, periods of great activity during which the Sultans, the Royal master-builders, the descendants of Alp Arslan, rivalled in the very heart of Asia Minor all the richness and artistry of the age of Pericles. The works of the great Seljuk Turks tell not only of local riches but of a time of prosperity during which the people had not only the leisure to produce their works of art but the encouragement as well. Food, naturally, took pride of place; where there is wealth the quality of food increases, and the great banquets of the early Turks produced many of the dishes we are still familiar with today. The whole roasted lamb or the young sucking calf stuffed with rice and exotic herbs, whilst never diminishing in appeal, gave way to more specialised dishes. The lamb and the calf were dissected and grilled chops (cooked over charcoal), kidneys ravished with butter and cream, kebabs wrapped in paper and cooked in pine kernels were discovered to have their appeal too. Rich in dress and ornamentation, succinct in speech, imbued with the knowledge of architecture – acquired undoubtedly in their migrations across Asia and half the face of the world – the early Turks liked their foods well spiced and highly seasoned. The spice trade originated with the Phoenicians; cane sugar was brought in by the Venetians in the Eleventh Century – the Turks, acquisitive, sampled everything.

Even today the Anatolian peasant lives somewhat better than his European counterpart. Turkey is still an agricultural country despite the reputation of her soldiers, and many of the regional dishes – Circassian Chicken, which comes to us from the mountainous Duzce, or Ankara Scoblianka, a product of the Tartars of old Ankara – come to us unchanged by time and are served in the hotels and restaurants (lokanta) of the big cities. Erzurum and Kars are regions rich in meat. Istanbul and the Black Sea coast give us fish unknown in any other part of the world. It might almost be said that life in Turkey revolves around food. Hours of long and patient effort are spent in the kitchens and in summer all meals are served in the open. Even in the shabbiest districts of old Istanbul each small house has its own veranda and its fig tree and perhaps an ancient vine or two and honeysuckle (most delicately named by the Turks 'hanim elli' – lady's hand) smothering the wire fences between the houses. Roughly hewn wooden tables are covered with fine linen cloths, relics of a great grandmother perhaps or made for the trousseau when the present middle aged housewife was a newly betrothed girl of ten. Cloths, napkins, cushion covers are all heavily embroidered in exquisite patterns; rich Sparta carpets cover the floors even though there may scarcely be a stick of furniture to stand on them. It is a land of carpets and prayer rugs and no Turkish family would ever be put to the shame of being without one or the other. Table arrangements differ from the European. Knives are used only for meat, all other dishes are eaten with a fork or spoon. Meat and vegetables are quite distinct dishes, each with its own honour, and are served as separate courses.

In this book it will be seen that some vegetable dishes are served cold. In Turkey this always applies to any vegetable which has been cooked in olive oil. Meats, kebabs, chops, steaks, are regarded as being best when eaten alone and even pilav, king of dishes, is handed separately. Very rarely, excepting in some of the French-inspired cooking, does pilav accompany the meat on the same plate.

Marketing is done daily and in the mornings, thus ensuring a continuously fresh supply of all perishable commodities. The markets are in the open and prices highly competitive – in a land of fruit, fruit is naturally very cheap. It is a hot country too (and therefore not immune to the dangers of cholera or dysentery) and being Muslim in character, the people are most fastidious about cleanliness. All fruit is washed before being eaten – even a bare-footed street urchin, hungry as a wolf more than likely, will not eat the piece of melon or peach that he has picked up beside a fruit seller's stall until he has first washed it in the fountains of the local mosque. The fish markets are colourful, noisy with the cries of the vendors and gay with the rigging and the bright sails of the little fishing smacks. The fishermen wear gaily striped aprons and murderous knives attached to a broad leather belt in the middle. The markets stretch along the shores of the Golden Horn, where the mosques of the city reflect their sad nostalgic shadows and the sky in spring and summer is vivid cerulean. Here is a riot of colour and harmony – worth any visitor's attention if he doesn't mind getting his feet wet. The fish, freshly caught, lie in silver state, their scales a glistening iridescence, bright yellow lemons and emerald green parsley arranged symmetrically around them. Some of the fish look mysterious – blue and rose enamelled – too exotic to be subjected to dissection in the kitchen. The swordfish (kiliç) sherry brown, the mullet (barbunya) glitteringly orange silver, the kalkan with its unexpected lime green bones and exquisite white flesh, the mackerel (uskumru) like a pearl in its bed of vines leaves, tufts of curly endive decorating it with artistry, give intellectual nourishment as well as, later perhaps, physical.

Freshly killed meats come to the cities two and three times in a week and to render them less tough, the Turks pound them thin with a heavy mallet then steep them in onion juice for a day or two until the meat has tenderised.

Pastrycook shops dominate city, village and town – next to the local coffee shops, where old men sit mulling over the day's news, they are the most popular innovations of Turkish community life. It is almost agonising to choose where to buy one's baklava or lokma, each little shop seems to have a more mouth-watering display than the next. These shops are famous throughout the land, often being handed down from father to son for generations and the secrets of sweet-making guarded jealously. Bayram days (religious festivals) have their own traditional sweets – of which baklava is the king. But Turkish Delight (lokum) and kadingobeği (lady's navel) are close seconds. Lokma is exclusively the going-to-school-for-the-first-time sweet; in the old days, perhaps, it was hoped to induce a sweet temper in the Imam who was the teacher. Imams were reputed men of notoriously short tempers and incredible meanness – witness the delightful name of Imam Bayildi – literally, the Imam Fainted – called thus because the original Imam for whom the dish was created is said to have fainted at the expense of the olive oil used in the making. Helva has less happy associations, being used on the fortieth day after a member of the family's death when, according to Muslim belief, the chin of the deceased drops. This, it is believed, causes great pain, so in order to lessen the pain special family prayers are said on that day and helva eaten in the name of the dead person. In the houses of the wealthy great pots of helva are made and distributed amongst the poor. In this way it is hoped more prayers will be said and the dead will have nothing to complain about.

There is another popular sweet called Aşure and here I shall be forgiven, I trust, if I quote shortly from my book *Portrait of a Turkish Family*. 'Aşure is a sweet cooked with wheat, beans, figs, sultanas, dates, what you will, the whole being boiled for several hours until the result looks a little like aspic jelly. The legend of aşure is that when Noah in the Ark found himself running short of supplies, he ordered all the remaining food to be cooked together for one last gigantic meal. This was aşure – or so we are told. During the days of the Ottoman Empire a month used to be set aside each year for the making of aşure in all the houses of the rich, who afterwards distributed it to the poor. When my grandfather was alive it used to be made in our house, fat Hacer being an adept at it. . . ' I remember it used to be made in a huge silver pot, copper lined, and for a whole day the house would be filled with the sweet, rather sickly smell of it. I have included it in this book rather as a relic of days that are gone and not in any expectation that a modern housewife will make it – even in Turkey today the practice has dwindled, excepting amongst the very old who are still concerned with the welfare of their souls.

The sheep too figures symbolically in Turkish life. On the first morning of every Kurban Bayrami the rich slaughter a ewe or a ram (if the latter its horns are painted silver and gold and a red ribbon adorns its throat) to give to the poor of their district in the belief that on the Day of Judgement the rams (or ewes) slaughtered throughout their life to feed the poor will carry them across the Sirat Köprösü – a bridge between earth and heaven, sharper than a sword and thinner than a hair.

Birds are immune. There is no Turkish recipe for the tongues of larks, for ortolans, or for stuffed pigeon – in fact the latter are considered to be the little messengers of God and enjoy great freedom in the gardens of the mosques where they strut and preen and are grotesquely overfed.

There are many Turkish dishes, but I have tried to include here only the ones most likely to appeal to the European palate. Even so the task has been difficult, for Turkish cooking *is* very rich. Dolmas are heavy with stuffing, cooked either in oil or butter. Meats, braised or grilled or cooked with a vegetable often come to table swimming in butter or sheep's fat. The famous Doner Kebab has been omitted (along with many other famous dishes) since modern kitchens do not contain charcoal stoves or a revolving roasting spit.

The names of the dishes are almost always expressive – such as Kadin Budu, literally lady's thigh or Kadingobeği, to be translated as Lady's Navel. The anatomy of the ladies has ever been a popular subject among the Turks.

It is with a certain pride, however, that I present this emasculated book of Turkish cooking, for many of the recipes are old family favourites – some of them were evolved by the 'fat Hacer' now, alas, dead and for whom I too ate helva hoping to lessen her pain in the new world. But all the recipes are old – even Hacer did no more than play upon a tradition – and the eating of a good plain pilav differs in no appreciable wise today from the days when, from across the fat rich pasturelands of Asia Minor, Sultan Mehmet in 1453 broke down the door of the Eastern Roman Empire.

It only remains for me to thank the many Turkish friends who yielded family secrets and also to add a special word of praise for my sister, Madame Muazzez Aretikin and my sister-in-law, Madame Bedia Orga, both of Istanbul, who have had the thankless task of testing a good many of these recipes.

Istanbul and London, 1955

SOUPS
CORBARLAR

ALMOND SOUP

BADEM CORBASI

½ lb ground almonds (*sweet*)   6 bitter almonds
4 cups veal stock   2 cups single cream
1 teaspoon coriander seed   6 large eggs
1 teaspoon lemon rind   1 teaspoon verbena salt

Hard boil the eggs, remove the yolks and put in a mortar with the ground almonds and the bitter almonds, lemon rind and coriander seed. Pound thoroughly to a paste and mix with 1 ladle of stock.

Put the rest of the stock in a stewpan and bring to the boil. Add the ground almond mixture, stir well and cook for 10 minutes on a low heat. Just before serving add the cream, reheat thoroughly but do not allow to come to the boil again.

CREAM OF CHICKEN SOUP

TAVUK CORBASI

1 *whole cooked chicken breast*	2 *cups milk*
3 *cups chicken stock*	1 *cup single cream*
4 *tablespoons butter*	6 *asparagus heads*
3 *tablespoons flour*	2 *tablespoons minced chives*
salt to taste	

Snap off the tough stalks of the asparagus and remove the
scales if sandy or tough. Plunge upright, tied together loosely,
into boiling salted water in a deep saucepan and cook for
20–25 minutes. Remove from heat, drain and keep hot.

Melt the butter in a pan, add flour (sifted), salt, milk and
stock and bring slowly to the boil, stirring frequently. Boil for
2 minutes, then remove from heat.

Put two-thirds of the chicken breast in a mortar and pound
into a paste. Add to the stock mixture and force through a
sieve. Return to the heat and add the cream. Heat thoroughly
but do not allow to boil again. Decorate with the rest of the
breast cut into fine strips, the asparagus heads and the minced
chives. Serve at once.

CIRCASSIAN SOUP
CERKES CORBASI

3 cups sifted flour
1 egg
3 egg yolks
2 teaspoons verbena salt
6 cups chicken stock
2 cups single cream
3 cups cooked minced chicken
3 large onions

1 teaspoon white pepper
4 sprigs parsley
4 tablespoons butter
1 tablespoon finely chopped mint
½ tablespoon fresh thyme
  (chopped)
½ teaspoon salt

Melt the butter and sauté the chopped onions until transparent. Add the chicken, parsley, verbena salt and pepper and cook another 5 minutes. Remove from heat and cool.

Sift the flour and salt into a mixing bowl, make a well in the centre and add 1 egg yolk, the whole egg and a very little lemon water (½ lemon juice and ½ iced water). Mix well and knead into a stiff dough. Cover the bowl with a damp cloth and leave the dough to 'rest' for 1 hour.

Roll out fairly thickly on a floured board. Now place the chicken mixture in teaspoonsful along the pastry, 1 inch in from the top edge and ½ an inch apart from each other. Fold the pastry over, seal with water and cut into squares. Repeat the operation until all the pastry and chicken mixture has been used.

Bring stock to boil, drop in the squares of pastry and simmer for 20–25 minutes with the lid on all the time.

Beat the remaining 2 egg yolks, combine with the cream and add to the soup at the end of the 25 minutes. Stir once, remove from heat immediately and serve with a garnishing of butter to which the thyme and mint have been added.

MEAT BALL SOUP
KOFTE CORBASI

1 lb finely minced lamb
  (uncooked)
1 onion (minced)
¼ cup rice
1 tablespoon butter
1 teaspoon each cayenne
  pepper and verbena salt
a little water

4½ cups consommé or bouillon
1 cup wine (white if consommé
  used, red if bouillon)
2 egg yolks
juice of 1 lemon
8 sprigs minced parsley

Put the stock into a pan with the wine, bring to the boil and reduce, uncovered, until only 4 cups of liquid is left. This will take some time, so reduce to the proper amount well beforehand.

Clean and wash the rice and boil for 15 minutes in plenty of boiling salted water. Strain and allow to cool.

Into a mixing bowl put the lamb, onion, cayenne, salt and cooked rice and mix well together with the hands. Shape into small balls, the size of a walnut, between *wet* palms and roll in the minced parsley. Arrange in layers in a stewpan and pour over them the wine and stock mixture and the butter (melted). Boil gently for 30 minutes, then remove from heat. Mix the lemon juice with a very little water (about 1 tablespoon). Beat the egg yolks and combine gradually with the lemon juice. Pour this into the stewpan, away from the heat and off the boil, sprinkle over the remaining parsley and serve immediately in consommé bowls.

ONION SOUP
SOĞAN CORBASI

8 *cups chicken stock*
1 *lb onions (chopped finely)*
3 *tablespoons butter*
½ *cup sifted flour*
1 *cup single cream*

½ *cup grated Gruyère cheese*
2 *tablespoons lemon verbena*
  salt
croutons of fried bread

Put the stock in a deep stewpan, add the onions and bring to boil. Simmer until the onions are soft, about 40 minutes. Strain through a sieve, forcing the onions through, and return the purée to the stewpan.

Melt the butter and add the flour, stirring all the time, and make a roux. Cook for 2–3 minutes. Thin down gradually with some of the stock, taking care that the mixture does not become lumpy. Add the cream gradually and pour the whole into the purée, mixing thoroughly. Pour into individual cups, sprinkle with the Gruyère and brown very quickly under the grill. Serve with the croutons of fried bread.

PALACE SOUP

SARAY CORBASI

1 lb button mushrooms
2½ cups turkey stock
1 cup single cream
1 cup white wine
2 tablespoons flour
croutons of fried bread

5 egg yolks
¼ teaspoon white pepper
1 teaspoon celery salt
2½ tablespoons butter
3 tablespoons minced chives

Melt 1 tablespoon butter, add flour and brown slightly. Add the stock by degrees, stirring all the time.

Slice the mushrooms in half and sauté in the rest of the butter. Add to stock and bring to boil slowly. Cook for about 40 minutes over a low heat. Remove from heat and add cream.

Beat the egg yolks, add wine and pour into the stewpan. Simmer for 1–2 minutes and serve at once with croutons of bread rolled in minced chives.

RED LENTIL SOUP
KIRMIZI MERCIMEK CORBASI

8 *cups veal stock*
1¾ *cups red lentils*
2 *onions (chopped)*
1 *teaspoon paprika*
4 *tablespoons minced parsley*

1 *tablespoon flour (sifted)*
3 *egg yolks*
2 *tablespoons butter*
¼ *cup wine vinegar*
1 *cup single cream*

Melt 1 tablespoon butter and fry the onions for 2 minutes. Add the cleaned lentils and 2 cups of water and boil until the lentils are tender (if more liquid is needed, use stock). Add stock, salt and paprika, bring to boil, then remove from heat. Strain through a sieve, forcing lentils through, return to pan and keep hot.

Make a roux with the rest of the butter and the flour and cook about 2 minutes. Add the cream very gradually, away from the heat, stirring all the time. Add the well-beaten egg yolks and combine this mixture with the purée. Do not heat any further but serve immediately, garnished with the croutons of bread rolled in the minced parsley.

Spoon over the wine vinegar at the table.

TRIPE SOUP
ISKEMBE CORBASI

2 lb sheep's tripe
1½ lb cow's tripe
8 cups water
rind and juice of 1 lemon
3 cloves garlic
½ cup veal stock
1 tablespoon butter
salt to taste

2 egg yolks
3 tablespoons dry white wine
3 teaspoons paprika
1 teaspoon sweet marjoram
⅛ teaspoon thyme
½ cup single cream
2 tablespoons sifted flour

Scrape, clean and wash the tripe very thoroughly and cut into large pieces. Put into a stewpan with the lemon rind, herbs, garlic and salt. Cover with hot water, bring to boil then simmer for about 6 hours, skimming from time to time, and adding more *hot* water if necessary. Remove the tripe, cool slightly then cut into 1-inch pieces. Strain the liquid in which it was cooked through muslin, then add the cubes of tripe and reheat very slowly. Melt the butter, add flour and cook 1 minute, stirring all the time. Remove from heat and thin with a little of the veal stock. Stir in the well beaten egg yolks and add the lemon juice, a few drops at a time, stirring continuously. Add to the stewpan, mix well, raise the heat a little and bring to the boil. Remove at once from heat, add the wine and a few pieces of mashed garlic, if liked.

Melt another 2 tablespoons of butter and when just sizzling add the paprika. Remove from heat and combine well.

Serve the soup in earthenware bowls with the butter/paprika mixture spooned over them.

WEDDING SOUP
DUGUN CORBASI

1 *lb mutton*
2 *lb marrow bones*
12 *cups water*
6 *tablespoons butter*
1 *lemon*
1 *teaspoon salt*
½ *cup white wine*

¾ *cup flour*
1 *large carrot*
1 *large onion (chopped)*
3 *egg yolks*
2 *teaspoons paprika*
1 *teaspoon cinnamon*

Trim and wipe the meat and marinate in the wine for 6 hours. Drain off and put into a large stewpan with the broken marrow bones, the carrot and the chopped onion. Add the water and the wine in which meat was marinated. Simmer very gently for 4 hours, removing all scum as it rises to the top. Remove the meat and bones and strain stock into another stewpan. Cut the meat into strips, julienne fashion, and add to the stock.

Melt 3 tablespoons of the butter in another pan, add the sifted flour and cook gently for 3–4 minutes, stirring continuously. Do not allow the flour to brown. Remove from heat and thin gradually with a little of the stock, taking great care at this stage that no lumps form. When it is thinned sufficiently, pour into the meat stock and stir well. Bring slowly to the boil.

Whisk egg yolks with the salt, add the juice of the lemon gradually and one or two ladles of stock. Stir well. Remove stock from heat, allow to go off the boil then add the egg mixture, combining well.

Melt the rest of the butter and mix in the paprika.

When serving the soup, spoon the butter and paprika mixture over each bowl and dust with cinnamon.

FISH
BALIKLAR

BAKED BASS

LEVREK BALIGI GRATAN

2–2½ lb whole bass
1 bay leaf
3 tablespoons butter
¼ cup grated cheese
salt and pepper to taste

1½ cups white wine
1 root of parsley
1 tablespoon flour
1½ teaspoons paprika

Clean the inside of the fish and wash well. Put them in a greased baking tin, pour the wine over them and add the crushed bay leaf and parsley root. Cook in a hot oven – 400° – for 50 minutes, turning after 25 minutes and basting frequently with the wine. Remove from the oven, take out fish and leave to keep warm.

Melt 1 tablespoon butter, add the flour and cook until slightly browned, about 3–4 minutes. Add the rest of the butter and stir until smooth. Remove the bay leaf and parsley root from the liquor, strain, and add this to the flour and butter, stirring all the time. Cook until thick. Add the paprika and the cheese, stir well and cook another 2 minutes. Remove from heat and spread this mixture over the fish. Brown under grill and serve immediately.

CARP IN WINE
SARAPLI SAZAN BALIGI

2 carp
½ cup tarragon vinegar
¼ cup sultanas
½ cup red wine
salt and pepper
parsley

1 onion (chopped)
6 or 7 peppercorns
¼ cup finely chopped walnuts
1 tablespoon lemon juice
enough fish stock to cover fish

Clean and cut fish into pieces. Salt each piece, smother with onion juice and leave in a cool place for 1 hour.

Cook the pieces of fish in the fish stock on a low heat until tender – this will not take very long as carp is a soft fish. Remove the fish and keep warm.

Add to the stock the sultanas, walnuts, wine and lemon juice and heat through, then boil rapidly and reduce liquor by half. Pour over the fish and serve garnished with thin lemon slices and chopped parsley.

RED GURNET

MERCAN BALIGI

2 lb red gurnet
½ cup wine
24 shrimps (cooked)
1 tablespoon sorrel
2½ cups water
1 cup single cream
1 cup grated cheese
salt and pepper to taste

6 tablespoons butter
½ cup button mushrooms
1 onion
½ bay leaf
2 tablespoons flour
½ cup water
1 carrot (diced)

Clean and fillet the fish and cut into 6 pieces. Wash well and arrange at the bottom of a greased saucepan.

Put the heads, bones and tails into a separate saucepan with all vegetables, excepting mushrooms. Add the 2½ cups water and cook at a simmer for 2½ hours. Strain and keep the liquor in a warm place.

Skin the mushrooms and add to the fish in the saucepan, add wine and fish stock and cook for 20–25 minutes on a moderate heat. Remove the fish and the mushrooms and reduce the liquor by half by rapid, uncovered boiling. Strain and keep hot.

Melt 1 tablespoon butter and fry the flour in it for 3 minutes. Add the cream gradually, stirring all the time, then add the reduced stock by degrees. Cook until nicely thickened, stirring all the time. Add the rest of the butter and stir again. Add cheese and seasoning and cook for 2 minutes, still stirring. Remove from heat.

Skin the fish and separate into small pieces, add shrimps, mushrooms and half the cheese sauce and mix well. Arrange in a serving dish in the shape of a fish and spread the rest of the sauce over it. Sprinkle with a little more cheese and brown under a grill. Serve hot.

MACKEREL IN OLIVE OIL
USKUMRU PILAKISI

4 *medium-sized mackerel*	*¾ cup olive oil*
5 *cloves of garlic (halved)*	*1 teaspoon paprika*
5 *onions (sliced thinly)*	*1 carrot (sliced thinly)*
1 *tablespoon tomato ketchup*	*1½ cups fish stock*
½ *cup white wine*	*salt to taste*

Scale and clean the insides of the fish. Do not remove the heads or tails. Heat half the oil in a wide-bottomed pan, add onions and cook for 15 minutes over medium heat. Add the carrot and garlic and cook a further 15 minutes. Remove pan from heat and add the rest of the oil, paprika, tomato ketchup, wine and seasoning, cover and cook another 20 minutes on moderate heat. Uncover and let boil fiercely for 7 minutes to reduce liquor, and remove from heat again. Strain through muslin.

Arrange the mackerel side by side in the liquor, cover with a napkin and then put on the lid. Cook on medium heat for 20–25 minutes then remove from heat and allow to cool in the pan.

Serve very cold.

B

STUFFED MACKEREL
USKUMRU DOLMASI

4 *large mackerel*
3 *eggs*
6 *sprigs dill*
2 *sprigs fresh mint*
¼ *cup dried blackcurrants*
   (*fresh can be substituted*)
1 *cup breadcrumbs*
½ *teaspoon coriander seed*

2 *cups olive oil*
1 *lb onions*
6 *sprigs parsley*
¼ *cup pine kernels*
1 *cup flour*
2 *teaspoons mixed herbs*
salt and pepper

Clean out the insides of the fish and wash well. Starting from the tail, rub the fish upwards with two fingers, exerting slight pressure all the time but taking care not to break the skin. Continue like this until the flesh inside has worked itself loose from the skin. Make a very small incision in the throat of the fish and through here work out the loose flesh and the backbone. It is during this part of the operation that care should be taken not to break the tender skin of the fish. Remember that to disembody the fish, pressure should be exerted *gently* from the tail upwards.

When the fish skins are completely emptied throw away the bones and chop the flesh into small pieces and put aside.

Put half the olive oil in a pan and fry the chopped onions until slightly browned. Add the pieces of fish, pine kernels, blackcurrants, mixed herbs, coriander and seasoning and cook for 6–7 minutes. Add the chopped dill, parsley and mint, mix well and remove from heat. Allow to cool slightly then stuff the skins of the fish with this mixture – tightly and firmly but not too bulging or the skin will break. Then pull down the head of the fish slightly so that the incision in the throat is partly covered and the stuffing will not escape in the cooking.

Roll the stuffed fish in flour, then in beaten egg and lastly in the breadcrumbs. Fry them in the rest of the olive oil on a low heat until both sides are a rich golden brown.

Serve when completely cold.

GREY MULLET
KEFAL BALIGI KAGITTA

6 small grey mullet
½ cup button mushrooms
   (halved)
1 carrot (diced)
½ cup fish stock

greaseproof paper
¼ cup olive oil
white part of 1 leek (chopped)
1 cup white wine
salt and pepper to taste

Grease a baking tin with butter.

Clean out the fish well, wash, and from the head downwards slit the back and remove the backbone carefully. Wash again, pat dry and lay side by side in the baking tin.

Heat the oil and fry the mushrooms, carrot and leek for 4–5 minutes. Add the wine, stock, salt and pepper and cook for about 20 minutes or until the vegetables are tender. Remove the vegetables and put on the fish, cover with double greaseproof paper and cook at 350° – moderate oven – for 20 minutes.

Reduce the liquor by two-thirds by rapid, uncovered boiling, strain and just before serving pour this over the fish.

RED MULLET
ĶAGITTA BARBUNYA

6 medium-sized red mullet
¼ cup olive oil
4 sprigs chopped parsley
greaseproof paper

6 tablespoons butter
juice of 1 lemon
verbena salt

Clean, wash and pat the fish dry, leaving on the heads and tails. Make a small slit in one side and clean out the insides thoroughly, wash well under running water.

Take double greaseproof paper and brush well with melted butter. Wrap the fish in this, secure with string, place on a baking sheet and cook in a hot oven – 400° – for 40–50 minutes.

Mix the parsley, lemon juice, olive oil and salt and sprinkle over the fish just before serving.

STUFFED MUSSELS

MIDYE DOLMASI

24 *large mussels*
1 *cup olive oil*
1 *large tomato (skinned)*
1 *tablespoon blackcurrants*
  (dried)
1 *teaspoon white pepper*
½ *teaspoon coriander seed*
½ *teaspoon fresh thyme*
  (chopped)

salt to taste
1 *cup rice*
1 *lb onions (chopped)*
1 *tablespoon pine kernels*
½ *teaspoon sugar*
1 *teaspoon chervil (chopped)*
½ *teaspoon poppy seed*
½ *teaspoon basil (chopped)*

Clean the rice, cover with very hot water and leave aside until the water is quite cold. Wash several times under cold running water. Scrape and clean the mussels thoroughly then with a sharp knife open them. Clean off the hairs inside and after washing them leave aside in a tray of coarse salt.

Heat the oil and fry the onions for 6–7 minutes. Add the rice, pine kernels and salt, cover pan and fry for 20 minutes, stirring frequently. Add ½ cup water, tomatoes, blackcurrants, herbs and pepper, mix well, cover pan and cook another 10–12 minutes. Add sugar, mix and remove from heat. Stuff the mussels with this mixture and arrange in layers in a wide-based pan. Add 1 cup of water, cover pan tightly and cook over a medium heat for 30–35 minutes. Remove pan from heat and allow the mussels to cool in their own liquor.

Serve very cold but just before serving dry the outsides of the mussels in a napkin and brush them over with olive oil to make them shine.

SHRIMP SOUFFLÉ
TEKE BALIGI SOUFLESI

8 *tablespoons butter*
6 *egg whites*
6 *tablespoons milk*
½ *teaspoon salt*

6 *egg yolks*
6 *tablespoons flour*
4 *tablespoons double cream*
36 *cooked shrimps*

Heat the butter on a low fire, add the yolk of 1 egg and beat smooth. Add, one by one, beating well after each ingredient, 1 tablespoon flour and 1 tablespoon milk. Repeat the process until all the yolks, flour and milk have been used. Stir well once and add the cream and salt.

Beat the egg whites until holding a peak and fold in carefully.

Butter a soufflé dish, line with the shrimps and a little more than half fill with the egg mixture. Bake at a moderate heat – 330° – until set and pale gold in colour. Serve at once, taking care the soufflé does not fall.

MEAT AND POULTRY
ET VE TAVUKLAR

ANKARA SCOBLIANKA
ANKARANIN SCOBLIANKASI

1½ *lb veal steak*
1 *large onion* (*grated*)
1 *cup single cream*
dash of paprika

6 *tablespoons butter*
6 *mushrooms* (*sliced*)
mignonette salt
1 *tablespoon red or white wine*

Cut the veal into thin strips, julienne fashion, flour lightly and sauté in half the butter until tender, shaking pan frequently to prevent burning, and taking care the strips do not break.

Sauté the onion in remaining butter until transparent but not brown, add the mushrooms and cook another 7–8 minutes on moderate heat until the onions are pale brown and mushrooms well cooked. Remove from heat and leave aside.

Remove the cooked veal from the pan, add 1 tablespoon flour to the butter left in it and stir until smooth. Add the wine and salt and allow to bubble, stirring all the time to prevent lumps forming. Add the cream gradually and reduce the heat, stir until sauce thickens then add the onions and the mushrooms. Add veal last of all. Serve hot, sprinkled with paprika.

BEEF BALLS

KOFTE

1 *lb minced beef*
1 *egg*
1 *cup breadcrumbs*
1 *teaspoon garlic salt*
½ *teaspoon chopped dill*
clarified fat for frying

2 *egg yolks*
juice of 1 *large onion*
1 *teaspoon white pepper*
2 *tablespoons flour*
½ *teaspoon chopped sorrel*

Prepare flour, breadcrumbs and the well-beaten egg, in separate dishes. Mix and knead for 10 minutes all the other ingredients, including the egg yolks. Form into flattened balls, dip in flour, then egg mixture, then breadcrumbs and fry in sizzling fat on a very low heat until well browned (10–12 minutes).

Serve hot with plain pilav.

BEEF WITH MACARONI

DANA ETLI MAKARNA

2 *lb sirloin of beef*
1 *cup red wine*
5 *peppercorns*
2 *bay leaves*
2 *chopped onions*
salt and pepper

4 *tablespoons clarified suet*
   dripping
1 *cup hot bouillon*
2 *cloves of garlic*
1 *diced carrot*
3 *tomatoes* (*skinned and seeded*)
½ *lb macaroni*

Melt the fat in a deep stewpan and fry the sirloin for 10–15 minutes on a very high heat. Reduce heat, add carrot, onions, garlic, bay leaves and peppercorns and cook a further 10 minutes. Add tomatoes and cook another 5 minutes. Add wine and after 2 minutes add the bouillon.

Cook in oven for 2 hours at 275° (slow heat), turning the meat at the end of the first hour. Remove the meat, slice, arrange on a serving dish and keep hot. Strain the liquid and keep hot, having first reduced by half.

Throw the macaroni into boiling salted water and cook for 20–25 minutes. Strain, wash quickly under running water and arrange round the meat on the dish. Pour the reduced liquid over the macaroni and serve at once.

CHICKEN IN ASPIC
JELATINLI TAVUK

1¼ cups diced chicken (cooked)	½ cup mayonnaise
1 teaspoon salt	¼ cup toasted slivered almonds
¼ cup stuffed green olives	¼ cup black grapes
2 tablespoons gelatin	2 tablespoons white wine
2 cups boiling water to which has	1 cup mayonnaise
been added the rind of 1 lemon	½ cup whipped cream

Strain the water and lemon rind through muslin and dissolve the gelatin. Add the wine and leave aside to cool.

When partially set add the chicken, ½ cup mayonnaise, salt, almonds, olives and grapes. When partially set again pour into a tube mould (wetted) and chill until firm. Unmould on a serving dish and surround with crisped cos lettuce (use ice water for crisping) and endives. Fill centre of tube with cottage cheese balls (mix 1½ teaspoons chervil with 1 cup white cheese for this).

Serve with 1 cup mayonnaise mixed with ½ cup whipped cream.

TO MAKE MAYONNAISE FOR THIS DISH:

½ cup olive oil	¼ cup water
¼ teaspoon salt	¼ cup tarragon vinegar
⅛ teaspoon dry mustard	⅛ teaspoon sugar
2 medium heaped teaspoons flour	1 egg

Put dry ingredients in a saucepan, add vinegar and water, stir well, and cook over low heat until mixture starts to bubble. Boil for 2–3 minutes, stirring continuously. Remove from heat, cool thoroughly, add egg and beat well for about 1 minute. Add the oil gradually, beating continuously until all oil is absorbed. Chill before serving.

CHICKEN À LA BURSA
BURSA TAVUGU

1 *young chicken (2–3 lb)*
3 *large onions*
bunch of mixed herbs tied in
  muslin bag
2 *tablespoons single cream*
1 *tablespoon capers*

⅓ *cup olive oil*
2 *cups chicken stock*
1 *tablespoon flour*
½ *cup stuffed green olives*
1 *tablespoon chopped parsley*

Cut chicken in serving pieces and slice the onions. Heat oil to boiling point, reduce heat and add the pieces of chicken and the onions and fry until a pale golden brown. Add the stock and the herbs and cook very gently until the chicken is tender. Remove herbs and chicken.

Mix the flour with the cream, pour into the stock and cook for a few minutes, stirring all the time. Add garlic salt. Add the olives and the capers and cook for another 3 minutes.

Pour over the chicken and serve at once, garnished with parsley.

CIRCASSIAN CHICKEN

CERKES TAVUGU

1–3-lb chicken
1 cup chicken stock
2 large onions (quartered)
2 stalks white celery
4 tablespoons breadcrumbs
½ teaspoon chervil
1 egg

8 cups water
2 cups shelled walnuts
1 carrot (sliced)
1 teaspoon sage
½ tablespoon paprika
½ teaspoon basil
salt and pepper

Clean and draw chicken and put in a large saucepan with the onions, carrot, celery, herbs and salt. Bring to boil slowly, skimming frequently. Reduce heat and simmer for about 2¼–2½ hours until tender. Remove chicken, strain liquor and put aside.

Remove all meat from chicken and shred into very small pieces.

Pound the walnuts in a mortar, add 1 tiny onion (finely minced), paprika and breadcrumbs and mix well together, pounding thoroughly. Add the 1 cup of chicken stock very gradually and mix to a stiffish paste. Add the egg, unbeaten, and leave aside for 15 minutes. Add the shredded chicken and stir well.

Shape mixture into cutlets, dip in beaten egg and breadcrumbs and fry in a little hot butter until delicately browned on both sides. Serve hot.

CHICKEN CURRY
HIND TAVUGU

1 *large onion (chopped)*
1 *teaspoon green ginger*
3 *tablespoons butter*
6 *tablespoons single cream*
1–3-lb *chicken (boiled)*
3 *hard boiled eggs*
4 *tablespoons mint (chopped)*
2 *tablespoons parsley (chopped)*
salt and pepper to taste

1 *teaspoon mashed garlic*
2 *tablespoons curry powder*
2 *cups chicken stock*
4 *tablespoons mayonnaise*
2 *cups cold rice (cooked)*
3 *large tomatoes (skinned)*
2 *tablespoons dill (chopped)*
1 *sprig basil*
1 *tablespoon preserved ginger*

Melt the butter and fry the onion, garlic and green ginger until pale golden brown in colour. Add the curry powder, season and cook on a low heat for 3–4 minutes. Add the chicken stock, boil and stir until it begins to thicken slightly. Add the chicken (minced) and cook slowly until dry but not too dry – the mixture should be barely moist but not at the sticking stage.

Allow to cool, mixing in the preserved ginger when half cool.

Mix in the cream and the mayonnaise and put in a ring mould and chill until set. Serve well chilled with plain boiled rice and garnish with the sliced eggs, sliced tomatoes and the fresh herbs, finely chopped. Fill the centre of the mould with pitted black olives and a little more preserved ginger, all sprinkled with lemon juice.

CHICKEN MACARONI
MAKARNA TAVUKLU

½ lb macaroni
6 tablespoons butter
4 slices of tongue
1 cup single cream
1 teaspoon white pepper
½ cup green peas (cooked)
salt to taste
½ cup buttered crumbs

6 quarts water
breast of boiled chicken
2 tablespoons flour
sprig of rosemary
1 tablespoon grated fresh
   coconut
½ cup chopped mushrooms
   (boiled for 5 minutes)

Cook the macaroni in the boiling water for 20 minutes, strain, wash under hot water and leave aside to keep warm.

Melt half the butter, add flour and cook for 3 minutes without browning, stirring all the time. Add cream slowly and boil for 2 more minutes, taking care the cream does not stick. Add coconut and seasoning, stir well and remove from heat.

Cut the chicken breast and tongue into strips, julienne fashion, and add to the cream mixture. Add peas and rosemary, stir and leave beside the heat.

Grease a baking tray and arrange half the cooked macaroni in it, pour the sauce over and add the rest of the macaroni. Garnish with the mushrooms. Spread the buttered crumbs over the top, dot generously with butter and cook until golden brown in a very hot oven. Serve hot.

GRILLED CHOPS

PIRZOLA

2 lb lamb chops
1 tablespoon olive oil
garlic salt
1 tablespoon white wine

1 tablespoon fresh thyme
   (minced)
juice only of 1 onion

Clean and trim all the fat off the chops, then pound the meat until it is less than half its original thickness.

Arrange on a large plate and pour over them the wine, onion juice and oil. Sprinkle with the thyme and the garlic salt and leave aside for two hours in a cool place, turning them at the end of 1 hour. Drain but do not wipe. Grill until nicely browned on both sides (about 8 minutes).

STEAMED CHOPS
PATATESLI BUGU PIRZOLASI

2 lb lamb chops
3 tablespoons clarified fat
2 tomatoes (skinned)
½ lb potatoes
garlic salt to taste

½ cup flour
¾ cup thin consommé
1 large onion
1 teaspoon black pepper
2 tablespoons chopped dill

Clean and trim the chops and pound with an iron mallet until less than half their original thickness. Arrange in a layer in a wide-based stewpan.

Cut the onion into very thin slices and place on top of the chops, add the tomatoes (sliced), the potatoes cut into thin rounds and the dill. Season with the salt and pepper and add the consommé. Cover pan tightly. Make a thick pastry with the flour and a little water and seal the edges of the lid thoroughly. Cook over gentle heat for 20 minutes, then increase heat a little and cook a further 2½ hours.

Remove pastry from lid and serve hot after 7–8 minutes' 'rest'.

COUNTRYMAN'S KEBAB

BAHCEVAN KEBABI

2 lb leg of mutton
6 tablespoons butter
40 button onions
2 sliced carrots
2 large tomatoes (skinned)

1 cup fresh green peas
2 pimentos (cut up)
3 tablespoons dill (chopped)
3 cups bone stock
garlic salt

Cut the trimmed and wiped meat into small pieces. Melt the butter and cook meat over slow heat for 15 minutes. Add carrots, cover and cook for 1 hour, still on low heat, shaking the pan occasionally to prevent burning. Add the cut-up tomatoes, onions, pimentos, green peas and salt. Add 1 cup bone stock *every* 30 *minutes* and cook for 1¾ hours. Add the dill at the last minute, stir once and then serve.

NOTE: This dish is especially delicious if served in traditional Turkish peasant style – that is, adding a few spoonsful of fresh yoğurt at table and sprinkling lightly with paprika.

LAMB KEBAB EN PAPILOTTE

KAGIT KEBAB

2 lb leg of lamb
2 chopped onions
1 large tomato (skinned)
2 tablespoons chopped dill
2 carrots (diced)
½ lb margarine (for frying)
1 teaspoon white pepper

½ cup cooked green peas
2 tablespoons clarified fat
¼ cup dry white wine
2 tablespoons chopped thyme
2 potatoes
1 teaspoon mignonette salt
greaseproof paper

Cut meat into fairly large pieces and fry in the margarine until both sides are pink. Remove from heat and leave aside. Add onions, carrots, half of the dill, salt and pepper and cook over gentle heat for 25 minutes. Add the wine and tomatoes and cover with greaseproof paper. Cover stewpan with lid and cook for 1 hour more. Take out the meat and the carrots and keep hot, separately.

Cut potatoes into thin round slices and sauté for 5–6 minutes. Add them to the carrots, green peas and thyme.

Take some fresh greaseproof paper (cut more than twice the size of each piece of meat) and put a piece of meat in the centre. Cover with enough of the vegetables, pour over a little sauce from the stewpan, bring ends of paper together so that everything is well sealed and the sauce cannot escape and twist the ends securely.

Lay the envelopes of greaseproof paper on a baking tray side by side, sprinkle with a little water and bake for 20 minutes in a very hot oven. Serve hot.

KEBAB IN PUFF PASTRY

TALAS KEBAB

1 *lb puff pastry*
1 *cup chicken stock*
1½ *tablespoons butter*
1 *teaspoon white pepper*
½ *teaspoon tarragon (chopped)*
1 *large egg*

1 *lb boned chicken*
3 *onions (thinly sliced)*
1 *tablespoon tomato purée*
1 *teaspoon chervil (chopped)*
2 *tablespoons parsley (chopped)*
salt to taste

TO MAKE THE PASTRY (old Turkish recipe):

1 *lb flour (sifted 5 times)*
*just under 1 cup cold water with
    enough white wine to make up
    to 1 cup – this means about
    1 tablespoon white wine*

1 *lb butter in ½-lb blocks*

Remember that all utensils, ingredients and hands should be quite cold. First sieve the flour (this will be the 6th time) into a mixing bowl. Cut each ½-lb block of butter into 30 or 40 small cubes by cutting 4 or 5 times crossways, twice lengthwise and once right through the middle. Separate the cubes and with the tips of the fingers mix lightly into the flour. With a large silver (or metal) spoon mix in the water/wine mixture and stir all together until the mixture leaves the sides of the bowl. Turn out on a well-floured marble slab and rolling *away* from you all the time with small, quick forward movements, shape into an oblong. This is the most important part of the whole operation so make quite certain that every part of the pastry is rolled *evenly*. Take hold of the top two corners and fold down to within a third of the bottom edge. Now fold the bottom corners up to the top so that you have a neat slab of pastry, three layers in thickness. Turn the paste to the right – this gives you a folded edge on left and right sides and leaves the two open edges facing you and away from you. Roll out and fold again as before. Do this 6 times in all then put immediately in the refrigerator. Do not use before 5 hours and, if possible, leave overnight.

TO MAKE FILLING:

Melt butter in a stewpan and cut the chicken into long thin pieces and cook in the butter for 5 minutes. Add the onions, stir once, cover and cook for 15 minutes, shaking pan occasionally to prevent sticking. Uncover and cook a further 10 minutes. Add the stock, tomato purée and salt, cover and cook on a very low heat for 2 hours. Add pepper and all the herbs, stir well, remove from heat and cool.

Cut the puff pastry into small pieces and roll out to 6-inch squares. Place some of the chicken mixture in the centre of each square, fold pastry crosswise into triangular shape, seal with a little beaten egg and put on a lightly greased baking tray. Glaze with beaten egg and bake at 350° (moderate oven) for 30 minutes.

RABBIT KEBAB

TAVŞAN KEBABI

1 *plump rabbit*
1½ *cups red wine*
1 *cup olive oil*
1 *teaspoon white pepper*
2 *bay leaves (crumpled)*
5 *cloves*
6 *cloves garlic*

juice of 1 *large lemon*
1 *teaspoon salt*
1 *teaspoon mint*
3 *tablespoons finely chopped*
    parsley
5 *tablespoons butter*

Wash and clean rabbit and leave the liver on one side. Stud the rabbit with cloves and a few pieces of garlic.

Mix together 1 cup of wine, olive oil, mint, bay leaves and parsley and marinate the rabbit in this for 24 hours, turning occasionally. Remove rabbit, drain but do not dry and grill on a very large skewer for 1½ hours, turning continuously to avoid burning.

Melt the butter, chop the liver finely and add to the melted butter with the remaining garlic which must also have been chopped. Sauté for 2–3 minutes, shaking the pan to prevent sticking. Remove from heat, cool slightly and pound into a paste in a mortar. Add the rest of the wine gradually, the lemon juice, salt and pepper. Transfer to a stewpan and over a low heat bring to simmering point, stirring all the time with a wooden spoon.

Pour this sauce over the grilled rabbit and serve immediately.

SHASHLIK

ŞAŞLIK

2 lb leg of lamb
1 cup olive oil
1½ cups button mushrooms
skewers

4 finely chopped onions
6 large spring onions
salt and paprika

Clean the meat from the bone, remove skin and fat and cut into 1-inch cubes. (Incidentally, the bones, skin and fat in this dish and all the shish kebab dishes can be used as a basis for stocks.)

Marinate the meat cubes in olive oil, salt and paprika for 24–36 hours (the longer the better). Allow 6 pieces of meat to each skewer, half an inch apart, and grill 5–6 minutes, turning all the time.

Sauté the mushrooms in the olive oil which was used for marinating and serve as a garniture with the pieces of lamb. Cut the spring onions very small and scatter over the whole dish.

SHISH KEBAB I

ŞIŞ KEBABI

2 lb leg of mutton
juice of 1 large onion
shish kebab skewers

1 tablespoon olive oil
salt to taste

Clean the meat from the bones, remove skin and fat and cut into 1-inch cubes. Put in a bowl with the onion juice and the olive oil and leave for 3 hours. Allow 6 pieces of meat to each skewer, place them half an inch apart from each other and grill for 5–6 minutes, turning all the time. Remove from the skewer at table and serve with pilav.

NOTE: Sliced green peppers, tomatoes and onion rings may be served as a garniture but these *must* be grilled on separate skewers. If they are included on the meat skewer the meat becomes tough and this is the reason why so many shish kebab dishes served in restaurants outside the Middle East are tough and unpalatable.

SHISH KEBAB II

ŞIŞ KEBABI

2 lb leg of lamb
2 cloves of garlic pounded in a
   mortar

salt
1 cup dry white wine
2 tablespoons butter

Clean the meat from the bones, remove skin and fat and cut the meat into 1-inch cubes. Marinate in the wine and the pounded garlic for 6–8 hours. Allow 6 pieces of lamb for each skewer, half an inch apart from each other. Brush well with melted butter and grill for 5–6 minutes, turning continuously. Serve hot with stuffed tomatoes.

STRING KEBAB

KAYTAN KEBABI

1 lb leg of mutton (without fat or bones)
¼ cup dry white wine
¼ teaspoon mignonette salt
¼ teaspoon nutmeg
¼ teaspoon chopped rosemary
2 tablespoons butter
½ tablespoon chopped dill

1 large onion (grated)
¼ teaspoon white pepper
¼ teaspoon cinnamon
¼ teaspoon ground cloves
1 tablespoon grated coconut
2 tablespoons chopped parsley
1 bunch spring onions

Cut the meat into pieces – 3 inches long by half an inch wide. Put in a bowl and add onions, salt, pepper and wine. Mix well and leave aside for 12 hours. Put each piece of meat on a skewer and grill one side for 3 minutes and the other side for 2 minutes.

Mix together the melted butter, coconut, herbs and spices and whilst the meat is being grilled keep brushing with this mixture.

Serve hot sprinkled with parsley, dill and spring onions.

TAS KEBAB

2 lb leg of mutton (top part)
2 chopped onions
1 teaspoon white pepper
2 cups lamb or bone stock
3 tablespoons butter

2 tomatoes (chopped and
  skinned)
1 level teaspoon fresh thyme
  (minced)
salt to taste

Cut the meat, freed of fat, into small cubes, sprinkle with pepper and the thyme and leave aside for 4 hours.

Melt butter and fry onions for 5 minutes. Add meat, cover stewpan tightly, reduce heat to *very low* and cook for 20 minutes, shaking pan occasionally to prevent sticking but not uncovering.

Cut tomatoes small and add to the meat and onions, with salt to taste and 1 cup of stock. Cook on low heat for 2½ hours until meat is very tender, adding the remaining cup of stock at the end of the first hour of cooking.

For the last 15 minutes of cooking time, uncover, increase the heat and boil rapidly until the liquid is reduced to a few tablespoons.

Serve with pilav.

VEAL TAS KEBAB

DANA ETLI TAS KEBABI

2 lb leg of veal (top part)
1 cup dry white wine
2 tomatoes (skinned)
1 bay leaf
¼ teaspoon ground cinnamon
2 tablespoons fresh coconut
(shredded)

¼ cup chicken fat
2 minced onions
1 teaspoon pepper
¼ teaspoon ground cloves
¼ teaspoon minced thyme
1 teaspoon mignonette salt

Cut the meat into pieces the size of a walnut. Put in a stew-pan with the onions, salt, coconut, bay leaf, thyme, cinnamon, pepper and cloves. Mix well and leave for 2 hours in a cool place.

Melt the chicken fat and add to the meat cubes in the stew-pan. Sauté for 3–4 minutes, shaking the pan continuously. Add the cut-up tomatoes and the wine. Cover tightly and cook over a low heat for 4 hours.

Serve immediately with saffron pilav.

CHICKEN KOFTE
TAVUK KOFTESI

1 *lb cooked chicken breast*
4 *egg yolks*
4 *tablespoons flour*
½ *teaspoon sweet marjoram*
3 *slices tongue* (*lamb's*)
1 *cup butter*

1 *cup single cream*
3 *tablespoons butter*
½ *teaspoon white pepper*
6 *chopped mushrooms*
¼ *cup gruyère cheese* (*grated*)
salt to taste

Cook the mushrooms in boiling salted water for 10 minutes. Remove from heat, drain and allow to cool.

Mince chicken breast very finely. Melt butter (3 tablespoons), add flour and cook without browning for 3 minutes. Add the cream gradually, stirring all the time, the well-beaten egg yolks, cheese and salt. Cook, stirring continuously, until mixture is very stiff. Add the chicken, mushroom and tongue – the tongue cut into very small pieces. Mix well, remove from heat and leave aside to cool.

Take small pieces of this mixture, about the size of a walnut, shape into flattish balls and fry in hot butter (1 cup) until golden brown on both sides – starting with very low heat and gradually increasing.

Serve hot with plain pilav.

FRIED KOFTE

TAVADA KOFTE

1 *lb beef*
3 *slices stale bread*
2 *grated onions*
2 *cloves garlic*
¼–½ *cup chicken fat*
salt to taste

1 *teaspoon cayenne*
2 *eggs*
1 *tablespoon chopped dill*
3 *tablespoons gruyère cheese*
¼ *cup white wine*

Soak the bread in the wine, then squeeze out dry.

Put meat through mincer 3 times, add the bread and put through the mincer once more. Add all the other ingredients (excepting chicken fat) and knead for 10 minutes. Wet palms of the hands with the left-over wine and shape the meat mixture into small balls.

Heat chicken fat to sizzling point and put in the balls. Reduce the heat to very low and cook until both sides are well browned. This should take 25–30 minutes.

Serve hot with a border of plain pilav.

LADY'S THIGH KOFTE
KADINBUDU KOFTE

1 *lb lamb*
2 *tablespoons rice*
4 *tablespoons butter*
1 *teaspoon white pepper*
1 *teaspoon mignonette salt*
a little whipped cream

1 *onion (chopped)*
2 *tablespoons soft white cheese*
3 *eggs*
½ *cup dry sherry*
flowerlets of parsley

Fry the onion in the butter until transparent but not brown.
Add the sherry, salt and rice, cover and cook until the rice is
tender. Remove from heat. Put meat 3 times through the
mincer then transfer to a stewpan and cook over a low heat
until all the meat juice is extracted. Remove from heat and
add all the other ingredients, including the cooked rice, and
knead together for 5 minutes. Shape the mixture into slightly
flattened ovals (to resemble a thigh), roll in beaten egg and
fry in butter until well browned. Serve garnished with the
flowerlets of parsley and a rosette of whipped cream.

KOFTE ON A SKEWER

ŞIŞ KOFTESI

1 *lb minced lamb (uncooked)*
2 *eggs*
¼ *teaspoon finely chopped thyme*
1 *teaspoon garlic salt*

juice of 1 *large onion*
¼ *teaspoon white pepper*
2 *tablespoons olive oil*

Grease the skewer well by putting it through a piece of suet.

Mix all the ingredients well together (excepting the olive oil) and knead thoroughly. Grease the palms of the hands with the oil and shape the meat mixture into small sausages. Brush well with oil, thread carefully on the skewer and grill 6 minutes, turning continuously.

Serve garnished with chopped chives.

C

KOFTE IN TOMATO PURÉE

DOMATES SALCALI KOFTE

1 *lb minced mutton*	1 *teaspoon paprika*
1 *large onion (minced)*	6 *tablespoons butter*
2 *slices thick stale bread*	3 *large tomatoes (skinned)*
2 *eggs*	1 *cup flour*
6 *sprigs of parsley*	1 *teaspoon mignonette salt*
½ *cup cider*	*almond oil*

Soak the bread in a little cider for 5 minutes, then squeeze out dry. Into a mixing bowl put the meat, onion, bread, parsley, eggs, paprika and salt and knead well together for about 10 minutes. Oil the palms of the hands with almond oil and shape the meat mixture into small, flattened balls. Flour both sides.

Melt the butter and drop in the balls and cook until nicely browned over a low heat.

Add the chopped tomatoes and the remaining cider and heat through. Transfer to the oven and bake 30–35 minutes at 300° (moderate heat). Serve immediately.

CASSEROLE OF LAMB

KUZU GUVEC

2 lb shoulder of lamb
4 tablespoons butter
3 large potatoes (sliced
  thickly)
3 tomatoes (skinned and cut up)
9 spring onions (chopped)
1 pimento (chopped)
1 teaspoon sorrel (chopped)

6 or 7 nasturtium flowers
3 cloves of garlic
1 lettuce (torn to shreds)
4 tablespoons dill (chopped)
2 onions (sliced thickly)
1 bay leaf
½ cup red wine
salt and pepper

Cut the meat into fairly large pieces and put in an earthen-ware casserole dish with all ingredients, excepting nasturtium flowers. Cover with greaseproof paper before putting on the lid. Cook at 340° (moderate heat) for 2½–3 hours.

Serve garnished with the nasturtium flowers.

LAMB CHOPS

KUZU PIRZOLASI PANE

6 *lamb chops*
2 *tablespoons flour*
1 *teaspoon pepper*
3 *tablespoons clarified dripping*
3 *teaspoons paprika*
½ *teaspoon olive oil*

1 *large egg*
1 *cup toasted crumbs*
3 *tablespoons olive oil*
6 *tablespoons butter*
1 *teaspoon fresh thyme*
salt to taste
sprigs of parsley

Trim and clean fat from the chops and beat with an iron mallet until a little under quarter of an inch in thickness.

Have prepared in separate plates the flour, breadcrumbs and the egg, which should be beaten very lightly then mixed well with salt, pepper, thyme and the ½ teaspoon of olive oil.

Lightly flour both sides of the chops, dip in the egg mixture and coat with toasted crumbs. Put 3 tablespoons olive oil and 3 tablespoons fat into a pan and when sizzling put in the chops and fry until golden brown – about 5–6 minutes each side. Do not overcrowd the chops in the pan.

Just before serving pour hot melted butter mixed with the paprika over them.

Garnish with young spring onions and a few sprigs of parsley.

LAMB IN THE OVEN
KUZU FIRIN

2 lb leg of lamb
½ cup white wine
½ cup single cream
5 tablespoons butter
1 egg yolk (small)
salt and pepper

2 tablespoons flour
½ cup milk
6 large potatoes
2 eggs
¾ cup gruyère (grated)

Put the meat in a tin, pour wine over it and cook in a moderate oven for about 1 hour, or until nicely cooked, basting occasionally with the wine.

Boil the potatoes, skin and slice two of them and lay on a large meat tray. Mash the rest of the potatoes, add eggs and egg yolk, 2 tablespoons butter, ¼ cup of the cheese and salt and pepper. Put through a forcing bag and pipe into rosettes around the edge of the meat tray. Keep hot until meat is cooked.

Slice meat and arrange it over the sliced potatoes in the tray.

Melt rest of the butter, add flour and cook for 2 minutes over a low heat without browning. Add milk gradually, then the cream, stirring continuously until nicely thickened. Add rest of the gruyère and cook for 3 minutes more. Pour this sauce over the sliced lamb and put the tray under the grill. Cook until top is delicately browned and serve at once.

LAMB WITH PILAV
KUZULU PILAV

1 lb minced lamb
½ cup fresh orange peel
salt and pepper
2 tablespoons butter

3 tablespoons finely chopped
  walnuts
1 teaspoon ground allspice

Brown the mince with butter in a stewpan. Add the orange peel, walnuts and seasoning, mix well and cook over a low heat until the meat is very tender – about 25–30 minutes.

Pile in the centre of a hot dish and surround with a ring of plain pilav. Dust with allspice and serve at once.

ALBANIAN LIVER

ARNAVUT CIGERI

1 lb lamb's liver
½ cup flour
2 teaspoons paprika
garlic salt

2 large onions
6 sprigs chopped parsley
1 cup olive oil

Clean, trim and slice the liver into very small pieces (the size of a walnut) and wash under running water. Put in a bowl with 1 teaspoon paprika and mix well. Roll each piece in flour, then toss in a sieve to shake off the surplus flour. Heat the oil until sizzling and fry the pieces of liver for 1 minute only. Put aside.

Put 2 tablespoons of the hot oil in a separate pan, add the rest of the paprika, stir well and pour over the liver.

Serve cold with thinly sliced raw onions mixed with minced parsley.

NOTE: To serve Spanish onions raw, slice thinly and sprinkle with salt. Leave aside for 30 minutes. Squeeze the slices of onion and salt together until onions feel limp, then rinse several times under cold running water. Onions prepared in this way leave no unpleasant smell and are digested easily.

MUTTON RAGOUT
KOYUN

2 lb mutton
6 tablespoons butter
60 button onions
2 pimentos

3 cups white stock
1 cup cider
4 tablespoons minced dill
salt to taste

Wipe over the meat and cut into small pieces. Melt butter in a stewpan and when just sizzling add the meat. Cook slowly, turning occasionally for 15–20 minutes. Add the onions, the cut-up pimentos, salt and 2 cups of the stock. Cook gently on low heat for 2½ hours, adding the remaining cup of stock at the end of the first ½ hour and the cider 45 minutes before the cooking time is finished. Remove the pieces of meat and reduce the liquid to half by rapid boiling. Add dill and pour the whole over the pieces of meat. Serve immediately.

OX TONGUE

SIGIR DILI

1 ox tongue
3 sticks of celery
2 carrots (diced)
2 tomatoes (skinned and
  seeded)
½ teaspoon basil
1 cup red wine

8 cups water
3 chopped onions
5 tablespoons clarified suet
  dripping
1 teaspoon chopped rosemary
5 peppercorns
1 teaspoon garlic salt

Clean and wash the tongue and put in a stewpan with the water, carrots, celery, 1 onion, salt and pepper and cook very gently for 1¾ hours, skimming when necessary. Remove the tongue and skin it.

Melt fat and fry tongue for 15 minutes. Add the rest of the onions, the rosemary, basil and peppercorns and fry for 15 minutes more. Add the tomatoes and cook another 5 minutes. Add the wine and 3 cups of the strained liquid in which the tongue was cooked. Cover with a napkin and cook 2 more hours on a very low heat.

Remove the tongue, cool slightly and slice. Sieve remaining liquid, return to saucepan and boil uncovered until a thick purée is obtained. Pour this over the sliced tongue and serve hot with piped rosettes of potato purée.

PALACE CURRY

SARAY BIFTEK

2 lb best fillet of steak
3 cloves of garlic
sliced root ginger (size of
   large walnut)
2 tablespoons curry powder
3 tablespoons red currant jelly
1 tablespoon grated fresh
   coconut
1½ teaspoons mignonette salt
2 tablespoons sour apples
   (finely chopped)

1 tablespoon dates (finely
   chopped)
2 large onions
3 chillis (chopped)
3 tablespoons clarified beef fat
1 tablespoon curry paste
1 cup bouillon
½ cup coconut milk
juice of 1 small lemon
2 tablespoons seedless raisins
⅛ teaspoon dry mustard

TO MAKE COCONUT MILK:

Grate half a medium-sized coconut and put in a bowl with
1 cup boiling water. Cover and leave for 4 hours, then strain
through muslin before using.

TO MAKE THE CURRY:

Melt the fat in a large stewpan, slice the onions and the garlic
very thinly and fry without browning for 5–6 minutes. Add
the chillis and the meat, cut into 1-inch cubes. Brown a little –
about 3 minutes – then stir in the curry powder, the paste and
the ginger. Stir well and cook for 2 minutes. Add the grated
coconut, coconut milk, bouillon, red currant jelly, apples,
raisins and dates. Cover and simmer very gently for about
2 hours or until the meat is very tender. Just before cooking
time is over add lemon juice and salt. Serve hot with plain
boiled rice and pickled limes.

RABBIT ESCALLOPES

TAVŞAN

2 *large slices of back of rabbit*
  (boned and beaten into
  escallops)
1 *teaspoon garlic salt*
6 *tablespoons butter*
slices of thin cheese (gruyère
  or cheddar)

toasted breadcrumbs
4 *tablespoons red wine*
1 *teaspoon fresh rosemary*
  (chopped)
1½ *tablespoons flour*
beaten egg

Marinate the boned and beaten rabbit slices in the wine, salt and rosemary for 6 hours, turning at the end of 3 hours. Drain well. Roll in beaten egg and breadcrumbs and sauté in the butter for 9–10 minutes, then remove from butter and keep hot.

Add the flour to the butter left in the pan and stir until bubbly. Cook for 2–3 minutes, stirring all the time. Add the wine mixture in which the rabbit marinated and stir until smooth.

Place a thin slice of cheese on each escallop of rabbit and grill until the cheese is a golden brown. Arrange on a serving dish and pour the wine sauce over the escallops. Serve at once with plain pilav.

STUFFING FOR TOMATOES OR
GREEN PEPPERS

½ lb minced beef
¼ cup rice
½ cup bouillon
2 tablespoons dill (chopped)
salt

1½ tablespoons fat
2 tablespoons red wine
1 onion (finely chopped)
½ teaspoon white pepper
1 teaspoon parsley (chopped)

Melt fat and fry the onions until lightly browned. Add rice and bouillon and cook until rice is soft and all the liquid has been absorbed – about 10–12 minutes. Remove from heat and cool slightly. Add the minced beef, wine, dill, parsley, pepper and salt and knead for 5 minutes. This stuffing is now ready to be used.

NOTE: This stuffing to be used with dishes to be served hot.

STUFFED TURKEY

HINDI DOLMASI

1 *young turkey*
1 *cup water*
3 *onions (chopped finely)*
2 *cloves of garlic*
6 *sprigs of dill*
1 *tablespoon dried blackcurrants*
salt to taste
a little good stock

1 *cup rice (Patna)*
9 *tablespoons butter*
2 *carrots (quartered)*
1 *large tomato (skinned and chopped)*
1 *tablespoon pine kernels*
½ *teaspoon pepper*
½ *teaspoon basil*
1 *tablespoon red wine*

Put the cleaned turkey in a large saucepan with the water, 5 tablespoons butter, onions, carrots and garlic, cover and bring to boil. Remove from heat and put the saucepan into a hot oven. Keep cover on and baste occasionally, cooking until turkey is tender. For the last 10 minutes remove cover, baste and allow bird to brown. Remove from oven, put bird in a warm place and strain the fat and juice in the saucepan. Increase the amount to 1½ cups of liquid by adding good stock and 1 tablespoon red wine. Put this liquor aside as it will be used for the making of the rice stuffing.

In the meantime, cut up the liver and heart of the turkey into small pieces, sauté for 3 minutes in butter and leave aside to keep hot. Clean the rice and cover with almost boiling water and leave aside to get cold. Wash several times under running water and drain.

Melt 2 tablespoons of the butter, add 1 more onion finely chopped, add pine kernels and fry until both are nicely browned. Add rice and cook another 8–10 minutes on medium heat. Add the 1½ cups of liquor (left aside from the turkey), the blackcurrants, tomatoes, herbs and seasoning, cover and cook on a slightly reduced heat until all liquid has been absorbed by the rice – about another 12–15 minutes. Add the minced dill, the liver and heart, stir well and remove from heat. Stuff the turkey tightly with this mixture, place in a warm oven for 40 minutes, then serve at once.

PRESSED VEAL

DANA ROSTO

2 lb flank of veal
⅛ teaspoon sugar
⅛ teaspoon salt
½ teaspoon paprika
¼ teaspoon dry mustard

⅛ teaspoon white pepper
⅛ cup lemon juice
¼ cup olive oil
2 cloves crushed garlic

Pound the veal with a heavy mallet as thinly as possible and marinate in the above ingredients for 3 hours, turning every 20 minutes. Drain well and spread out flat. Sprinkle with:

1 onion (minced)
1 teaspoon allspice

salt and pepper to taste

Roll up tightly, sew ends with stout thread and tie in two or three places with string. Put meat in a deep saucepan of boiling water, adding:

1 onion (coarsely chopped)
1 bay leaf

1 stalk green celery

Simmer for 2–2¼ hours or until meat is very tender. Remove from water, drain and press in a long tin, cover with a napkin. Cover with a very heavy weight until it is cold.

Serve cut into slices with plain salad.

VEAL STEAK

DANA TAVASI

1 lb veal steak
1 cup tomatoes (skinned and chopped)
1 teaspoon salt
2 onions (finely chopped)
1 teaspoon chervil
¼ cup mushrooms (diced and sautéed in butter for 3 minutes)

5 tablespoons butter
1 bayleaf
1 teaspoon white pepper
1 leaf of rosemary
¼ cup double cream
½ cup buttered crumbs

Heat the butter and brown the veal steak (which should be cut into 1-inch cubes).

Add the tomatoes, salt and pepper, bayleaf, onion, rosemary and chervil and simmer until meat is very tender – about 55 minutes.

Turn the whole thing into a baking dish, add the cream, mushrooms and buttered crumbs and cook in a moderate oven for 15–20 minutes.

Finish off by browning crumbs under the grill and serve immediately.

VEAL STEAK WITH WINE
ŞARAPLI DANA

4 pieces of veal steak of 1 inch
thickness
4 tablespoons veal stock
Seasoned flour (¼ cup flour,
1 teaspoon garlic salt,

1 teaspoon paprika, sifted
together)
7 tablespoons dry white wine
4 tablespoons butter

Pound the steaks until the fibre is well separated and the steaks
are very thin. Season with salt and pepper and pour over them
4 tablespoons wine. Marinate 3 hours, turning after 1½ hours.
Drain but do not dry and dip each steak in the seasoned flour.
Brown both sides in butter over a fierce heat. This is for the
purpose of sealing the meat juices and should be done very
speedily.

Remove from heat when nicely sealed, add the stock and
the remaining 3 tablespoons wine, cover and cook very slowly
until tender.

Serve in its own juice with a border of white pilav cooked
in veal stock.

STUFFED BREAST OF VEAL
DANA GOGUS DOLMASI

2 *lb breast of veal (boned)*
2 *chopped shallots*
2 *beaten egg yolks*
1 *teaspoon chives (minced)*
1½ *cups of veal stock*
salt and pepper

2 *slices of stale bread soaked*
in veal stock
¾ *cup chopped mushrooms*
3 *tablespoons butter*
1 *teaspoon dill*
1 *large onion (minced)*

Pound meat to half its original thickness.

Mix the bread, shallots and mushrooms, add egg yolks and seasonings. Mix well and spread over the veal as evenly as possible. Roll and skewer tightly.

Heat the butter, add the veal and the minced onion and cook until the meat is well browned all over. Add stock and herbs, cover and simmer until the meat is tender – about 2¼ hours.

Serve hot in own juices.

HOT VEGETABLE DISHES
SICAK SEBZE YEMEKLERI

AUBERGINE CASSEROLE

OTURTMA

3 *large fresh aubergines*
½ *cup bouillon*
1 *large onion (finely chopped)*
½ *teaspoon white pepper*

6 *tablespoons clarified fat*
½ *cup minced lamb (uncooked)*
3 *tomatoes (skinned)*
½ *teaspoon salt*

Fry the onions in 2 tablespoons of fat until transparent but not brown. Add the meat and cook a further 10 minutes. Add 1 of the tomatoes (chopped) and cook another 10 minutes. Add salt and pepper, stir, and remove from heat.

Cut off tops of aubergines and pare off skin in ½-inch strips lengthwise. Cut the aubergines in two, lengthwise, salt generously and leave aside for 30 minutes until all the bitter juice of the vegetable has been extracted. Wash thoroughly under running water and fry in the remaining fat until nicely browned on both sides.

Arrange the pieces side by side in a wide-bottomed pan, cut side upwards, and spread with the mince mixture. Arrange slices of tomato on top, add bouillon, cover and cook on medium heat for 30–40 minutes.

Serve hot in their own juice.

AUBERGINE

PATLICAN KARNIYARIK

4 aubergines
½ lb clarified fat
3 small onions (chopped)
4 green peppers
salt to taste

½ lb beef mince
1 cup bouillon
3 tomatoes (skinned and
   halved)
½ teaspoon pepper

Fry the onions in 2 tablespoons of fat until transparent but not brown. Add the mince and cook another 10 minutes. Add 2 of the tomatoes and the seasoning and cook until the tomatoes are a purée. Remove from heat. Prepare the aubergines in the same way as they were prepared for Imam Bayildi (page 114) but before filling them fry them in the rest of the fat until they are a very pale brown. Remove very carefully and lay them in a wide-bottomed saucepan, side by side. Fill the cut parts with the minced beef mixture and put a slice of tomato on the centre of each and thin strips of the green pepper on each end. Add the bouillon and cook over a low heat for 40–45 minutes. Dish up very carefully without breaking the aubergines.

NOTE: This dish is served as a main dish with plain pilav to follow, and salad.

AUBERGINE KEBAB
PATLICAN KEBABI

1 lb leg of lamb
2 tomatoes (skinned)
¾ cup white wine
salt and pepper

4 tablespoons butter
1 cup water
1 large onion
2 large aubergines

The aubergines should be smooth and shiny, quite unwithered-looking and of a dark purplish colour. Peel them lengthwise in strips, leaving a line of flesh between each section of purple skin. Cut into 1-inch thick slices and put into a bowl, sprinkling generously with salt, and leave aside for 30 minutes. This must be done with all aubergines in order that the bitter juice may be extracted. Wash several times under running cold water, dry in a napkin and plunge into the sizzling butter. Cook until both sides are nicely browned then remove with a draining spoon and put on one side.

Cut the meat into small cubes and sauté in the same butter – 2 minutes for each side. As each pan of meat is cooked transfer it to a larger stewpan which should be warming by the side of the cooker.

Peel onions and cut into thin slices, cut tomatoes and fry in the butter mixture (the meat will have left some of its own juice). Cook for 3 minutes, then add to the meat in the stewpan. Add the cooked slices of aubergine last of all and the salt and pepper to taste. Cover and cook on a very gentle heat for 2–2½ hours. *Do not* stir but shake pan occasionally. At the end of the first hour add the wine. Serve hot with plain pilav.

AUBERGINE MOUSAKA

PATLICAN MOUSAKKASI

1 lb minced beef steak
6 aubergines
3 tablespoons finely chopped
  onion
½ teaspoon sorrel
½ cup of milk
6 tablespoons grated cheese
salt and pepper

4 large tomatoes (skinned)
2 tablespoons butter
½ tablespoon finely chopped
  parsley
2 tablespoons flour
½ cup bouillon
butter for frying
½ cup buttered crumbs

Heat 2 tablespoons butter and fry onion for 3 minutes. Add the mince and cook until all the meat juice has been extracted and then absorbed again – about 20 minutes. Add the cut-up tomatoes and stock. Season, cover and simmer until the meat is tender – about 30 minutes. Add parsley and remove from heat. Melt another 2 tablespoons butter, add flour and cook without browning for 3 minutes. Add the milk gradually, stirring all the time, bring to boiling point and then add the cheese and simmer for 10 minutes, stirring to prevent any lumps.

Cut off stalks of aubergines, pare the dark outer skin lengthwise, leaving strips half an inch apart, and cut the vegetable into thick slices. Salt generously and leave aside to extract the bitter juices. After 30 minutes wash well and drain. Pat dry and cook in butter until each slice is golden brown on both sides, then drain on paper.

Grease a baking dish and arrange layers of meat and aubergine, finishing with a layer of aubergine. Pour over it the cheese sauce, sprinkle with a little more cheese and the buttered breadcrumbs and brown in a hot oven. Serve hot.

AUBERGINE SAUCE
PATLICAN SALÇASI

3 *fresh aubergines*
3 *tablespoons butter*
1½ *cups single cream*
¼ *teaspoon chives (minced)*

3 *tablespoons flour*
3 *tablespoons grated cheese*
mignonette salt to taste
½ *teaspoon lemon rind*

Melt the butter and cook the flour for 3 minutes over low heat without browning, and stirring all the time. Leave aside. Add salt, chives etc.

Grill the unpeeled aubergines over a fierce flame (hold by the stalk) and then peel off the burned skin which should flake off very easily. Cut the pulp into small pieces, add to the butter and flour and mash thoroughly. Return to moderate heat, add cream gradually and stir until the mixture is completely free from lumps. Add the cheese and stir again until quite smooth and velvety.

This sauce should be served hot with roast chicken.

AUBERGINE WITH WHITE CHEESE
PEYNIRLI PATLICAN

3 aubergines
4 large eggs
1 tablespoon minced dill
1 cup toasted breadcrumbs
1 cup olive oil for frying

1 cup soft white cheese
2 tablespoons minced parsley
1 teaspoon minced chives
½ teaspoon garlic salt

Remove tops of aubergines and peel skins in ½-inch wide strips lengthwise. Cut the aubergines into four, lengthwise and leave aside for 30 minutes, sprinkled generously with salt. Wash well, dry and fry in olive oil until pale brown. Leave aside to cool.

Mash the cheese with a fork, add salt, parsley, dill, chives and 2 of the eggs and mix well together. Spread this mixture over half the aubergines, cut sides upwards, and arrange the other half of the aubergines on top, sandwich fashion.

Beat the other two eggs lightly and roll the aubergine sandwiches in this and then in the toasted crumbs. Fry in olive oil for 6–7 minutes and serve hot.

BROAD BEANS AND LAMB

KUZULU BAKLA

2 lb fresh young beans
¾ lb boned lamb
1 tablespoon chervil (chopped)
juice of 1 small lemon
salt to taste
5 tablespoons butter

2 onions (chopped)
1½ cups white stock
2 teaspoons sugar
1 teaspoon crushed pine
    kernels

Cut the meat into small pieces and put in a stewpan with butter, onions, chervil, pine kernels and salt. Cover and cook for 30 minutes, shaking pan occasionally. Remove from heat and leave aside.

String the beans, wash and drain and mix with the lemon juice and add to the meat mixture. Add the stock and sugar, cover with greaseproof paper sprinkled with water, put on lid and cook 1½ to 2 hours until beans are very tender.

Serve hot in own liquor.

STUFFED CABBAGE LEAVES

ETLI LAHANA DOLMASI

I *lb white cabbage*
¼ *cup rice*
I *lb beef mince*
I *tablespoon tomato ketchup*
I *teaspoon salt*

4 *tablespoons clarified fat*
I *cup water*
2 *large onions*
I *teaspoon pepper*
I *cup bouillon*

Cut cabbage in half, lengthwise and take out the tender middle part (this can be used grated for salads). Wash remaining cabbage and put into boiling salted water and cook for 2 minutes. Strain off water and allow the cabbage to cool. Tear off leaves gently and cut into 4-inch squares. Melt half the fat in a pan, add the onions (finely chopped) and fry until pale brown. Add the cleaned rice and the bouillon and cook over a moderate heat until rice is tender – about 10–12 minutes. Remove from heat, add the mince and seasoning and knead all together for 5 minutes.

Take I teaspoon of this mixture and put on the centre of a square of cabbage, fold envelope fashion – bottom, top and sides – and arrange at the bottom of a shallow, wide-based kettle. Continue until all cabbage and filling has been used. Add the tomato ketchup and the rest of the fat and pour on half a cup of boiling water. Cover kettle with a plate with a heavy weight over it and cook for 35 minutes on moderate heat. Serve hot.

CABBAGE WITH LAMB

KUZULU LAHANA

2 lb cabbage
4 tablespoons butter
1½ cups consommé
salt and pepper

1 lb lamb
2 large onions (chopped finely)
2 pimentos (cut in strips)

Melt butter, add the onions and the lamb cut into small 1-inch cubes, cover and cook for 25 minutes, shaking pan frequently to prevent sticking.

Clean cabbage, discarding tough outer leaves and cut in small pieces. Add to meat and onions. Add salt and pepper and the pimento strips, cover and cook another 15 minutes, still shaking pan now and then.

Add the consommé, cover, and continue cooking on a very reduced heat for 2¼ hours.

Serve hot in own juice.

FRENCH BEANS WITH MEAT
ETLI TAZE FASULYE

2 lb beans
2 large onions (chopped)
2 tomatoes (skinned and
   seeded)
1 teaspoon mignonette salt

4 tablespoons clarified fat
1½ lb lamb or veal (with a
   little fat left on)
5 cups white or veal stock
1 teaspoon chopped rosemary

Cut the meat into small pieces. Melt fat and fry the onions for 5 minutes. Add meat and cook another 15 minutes on a moderate heat. Add the tomatoes, cut up, the stock, rosemary and salt. Cover tightly and cook about 1 hour on a low heat.

String and wash the beans and cut into strips. Add to pan and continue cooking until beans are very tender. Serve hot in own liquor.

HARICOT BEANS WITH LAMB

ETLI KURU FASULYE

½ lb haricot beans (small)   5 tablespoons butter
2 tomatoes (skinned)   1 pimento (sliced)
½ lb fatty lamb   2 onions (chopped finely)
3 cups white stock   salt and pepper
½ teaspoon fresh thyme   ½ teaspoon basil

Soak beans overnight in slightly salt water, strain and wash
well. Put into boiling water and cook for 25 minutes. Strain
and leave aside.

Melt butter and fry onions until transparent, add the meat
cut into small pieces and cook another 15 minutes, shaking pan
occasionally to prevent sticking. Add the chopped tomatoes
and pimento strips, seasoning, herbs and stock, cover and cook
on low heat for 45 minutes. Add the haricot beans and the
water in which they were cooked, and cook until the beans
are very tender but unbroken.

Should any more liquid be necessary (in case beans are old
and take too long to cook) add more hot water.

Serve hot with plain pilav.

LEEKS WITH MUTTON
ETLI PIRASA

2 lb leeks
3 tablespoons butter
1 large onion (chopped)
2 large tomatoes (skinned)
1 lb mutton

3 tablespoons rosemary
  (chopped)
1 cup white stock
salt and pepper

Cut meat into 1-inch cubes. Melt half the butter and add the onions and the meat. Cover and cook for 25 minutes, shaking pan occasionally to prevent burning. Add seasoning, sliced tomatoes and ½ cup of the stock, cover and cook on moderate heat for another 45 minutes. Remove from heat and leave aside.

In a separate stewpan melt the rest of the butter and add the washed, white part of the leek, cut into ½-inch slices. Add the rest of the stock, cover and cook on moderate heat for 20 minutes.

Add the leeks and liquor to the other pan of meat etc, and cook, covered, until the meat is tender – about 50 minutes on a moderate heat.

Serve hot in own juice, sprinkled with the rosemary.

MARROW WITH CHICKEN
TAVUKLU KABAK

3 young marrows
3 cups water
3 tablespoons flour
1 cup single cream
½ cup grated Parmesan
2 lb spring chicken

1 cup white wine
3 tablespoons butter
1 cup chicken stock
½ teaspoon white pepper
½ teaspoon salt

Put the cleaned chicken in a stewpan with the water, wine and salt and simmer gently for 2 hours, removing scum as it rises to the top. Remove chicken and by rapid, uncovered boiling reduce the liquor to 1 cup. Shred the chicken finely and leave aside.

Clean and scrape the marrows, cut in half lengthwise and remove all seeds. Leave in salt water for 10 minutes. Drain, cover with fresh water and boil about 35 to 40 minutes. Remove, drain, and arrange on a lightly greased baking dish, the cut parts uppermost.

Fry the flour in the butter over a low heat for 2–3 minutes. Add the reduced chicken stock gradually, stirring all the time, add cream and bring to boil very slowly. Add seasoning and half the cheese and cook for a further 10 minutes without browning. Pour half of this sauce over the shredded chicken and combine well. Spread the mixture over the marrows, pour on the rest of the sauce, add the remaining cheese and bake in a hot oven for about 15 minutes until top is nicely browned. Serve hot.

STUFFED MARROWS
KABAK DOLMASI

3 young marrows
¾ lb lamb (minced) without fat
1 teaspoon sweet marjoram
3 tomatoes (skinned and
    seeded)
¼ cup rice
½ tablespoon chervil (minced)
salt to taste

4 cups bouillon
3 tablespoons clarified fat
1 teaspoon white pepper
1 onion (chopped)
2 tablespoons minced parsley
½ cup white wine

Select fat young marrows. Scrape and cut off the bottom end.
Scoop out insides, discard seeds, and cover the marrows with
water and lemon juice and leave aside.

Put half the fat in a pan and cook onions until transparent.
Add the wine and the cleaned rice, cover saucepan and cook
for 10 minutes. Remove from heat and add the lamb, salt,
parsley, sweet marjoram, chervil and salt and pepper and cook
for 5–7 minutes. Add the marrow pulp to this and remove
from heat.

Drain and wipe the marrows and stuff tightly with the meat
mixture and place in a large saucepan. Add the rest of the fat,
½ cup bouillon, cover tightly and cook for 15 minutes on
medium heat. Add the cut-up tomatoes and the rest of the
bouillon and cook another hour. Serve hot in their own liquor,
decorated with dill.

D

YOUNG MARROWS

TAZE KABAK

2 young marrows
4 tablespoons butter
1 onion (chopped)
½ tablespoon dill (chopped)
1 teaspoon paprika
½ lb veal

2 cups veal stock
3 tomatoes (skinned and seeded)
½ tablespoon tarragon (chopped)
a little garlic salt

Cut the meat into small pieces, salt, add dill and tarragon and leave aside for 1 hour, turning at the end of 30 minutes.

Melt half the butter in a stewpan, add onions and meat and cook over low heat for 30 minutes, shaking pan occasionally. Add the cut-up tomatoes and cook for another 10 minutes, then remove from heat and leave aside.

Scrape and clean the marrows, cutting off each end. Cut into four, lengthwise, and remove the seeds. Cut into cubes of about 1 inch.

Put these into a pan with the rest of the butter and ½ cup of stock and cook on medium heat for 10 minutes.

Put meat and marrows into a tray in layers making sure that the top layer is of marrows. Add the rest of the stock (hot) and the liquor left from the meat and marrow stewpans and cover with greaseproof paper sprinkled with water. Put on lid and cook on medium heat until the marrows are tender – about 1 hour, depending on age of marrows.

Serve hot in its own juice and garnished with dill and tarragon, sprinkled with paprika.

OKRA WITH BREAST OF DUCK
ORDEKLI BAMYA

1½ lb okra
2 cups duck stock
3 large onions (chopped)
1 green pepper (sliced and seeded)
1 cup tarragon vinegar
1 large orange (sliced)

2 lb cooked breast of duck
2 tablespoons clarified fat
3 large tomatoes (skinned and seeded)
6 mushrooms (sliced)
½ cup red wine
salt and pepper

Cut the breast of duck into slices.

Melt fat and sauté the onions for 5 minutes, add the mushrooms and cook another 5 minutes. Add ½ cup stock and the slices of duck and bring to boiling point very slowly. Remove from heat.

Cut the bottoms and tops off the okra and wash well under running water. Put in a bowl, add vinegar and 2 *tablespoons* salt. Mix all together well and leave for 1 hour. Wash and drain several times, arrange in a dish, with the tomatoes (1 layer okra, 1 layer tomatoes etc, with the meat mixture as the middle layer and finishing with a layer of okra). Add the green pepper, the orange slices and salt and pepper, the wine and the rest of the duck stock. Cover and bring to boil, reduce heat to low medium and cook for 1¼ hours. During the last 10 minutes cook uncovered at a higher temperature so that the liquor is reduced and thickened. Serve hot in its own juice.

PEAS WITH LAMB
KUZULU BEZELYE

2 lb shelled peas
1 lb boned lamb
2 tablespoons dill (chopped)
½ teaspoon fresh thyme
  (chopped)
3 cups marrow bone stock

4 tablespoons clarified fat
2 small onions (chopped)
1 teaspoon sorrel (chopped)
½ tablespoon sugar
½ teaspoon celery salt

Cut meat into small pieces. Melt fat, add onions, meat, thyme, sorrel, half of the dill and the salt. Cover and cook for 30 minutes, shaking pan now and then to prevent burning. Add bone stock and bring to boil, skimming as necessary. Add sugar and peas and simmer 40 minutes or until peas are very tender but not 'mushy'. In the case of very young peas the cooking time will be considerably reduced.

Add the rest of the dill, stir once and remove from heat. Serve in own liquor as a main dish.

STUFFED GREEN PEPPERS
ETLI BIBER DOLMASI

6 *large green peppers*
1 *cup bouillon*
salt

2 *tablespoons good clarified fat*
2 *tablespoons chopped parsley*

Choose your peppers carefully. They should be medium in size and of a uniform shape, not too intensely green nor too yellow.

Cut out the stalk very carefully – this will act as your 'lid' later on – and be careful not to split the peppers. Clean out all the seeds and wash well under running water. Boil for 5 minutes, then strain this water off – this renders the peppers less bitter. Add fresh boiling water and boil for 5 more minutes. Strain and leave aside to cool.

Fill with stuffing Number 1 (see page 76), adding the stalk as cover. Stand upright in a stewpan, add bouillon, fat and salt and cook over moderate heat for 35–40 minutes. Serve hot in their own liquor and decorated with parsley.

POTATOES AND MINCED BEEF
KIYMALI PATATES

2 lb potatoes
6 tablespoons clarified fat
2 cups bouillon
1 green pepper (seeded and cut in strips)
1 teaspoon garlic salt
1 cup fat for frying
2 large tomatoes (skinned)
¾ lb minced beef
2 onions (chopped)
1 teaspoon pepper
½ cup sliced mushrooms

Pare the potatoes, wash them and cut into thickish slices. Leave in salted water.

Melt the clarified fat and fry the onions for 5 minutes. Add the mushrooms and cook another 3 minutes. Add the mince, salt and the slices of green pepper and cook another 15 minutes. Add the chopped tomatoes, remove from heat and keep warm beside the fire.

Sauté the potatoes in the cup of frying fat and when golden brown add to the other ingredients. Pour the bouillon over all and cook on a moderate heat, covered, for 20 minutes.

Serve hot.

STUFFED POTATOES
PATATES DOLMASI

3 lb large round potatoes
½ cup finely chopped tongue
4 tablespoon butter
½ cup single cream
minced parsley
2 slices cooked chicken breast

½ cup sliced button mushrooms
  (sautéed)
2 egg yolks
½ teaspoon pepper
  and ½ teaspoon salt

Choose well-shaped potatoes of the same size. Scrape and cut a thin slice off one end of each so that they can stand upright on a dish. Wash, dry and place on a greased baking sheet and bake in moderate oven – 350° – for about 30 minutes or until nicely browned. Remove from oven and cut a 'lid' off top end of each potato and scoop out insides, leaving a shell at least half an inch thick.

Take about ⅓ of the potato insides, add salt and pepper and mash with a fork. Add ½ the butter, the cream, yolks of eggs, chicken breast (minced), tongue and mushrooms. Mix well and fill the potato shells and put on covers. Arrange upright on a baking dish, brush with the rest of the butter, melted, and bake for 10 minutes in hot oven. Just before serving brush once more with melted butter and roll thoroughly in the minced parsley.

STUFFED TOMATOES
DOMATES DOLMASI

6 *large tomatoes*
1 *cup bouillon*
salt and pepper

2 *tablespoons butter*
6 *sprigs parsley*

Wash tomatoes and cut a 'lid' from the top of each. Clean out the pulp inside, taking care not to break the skins. Fill with Stuffing Number 1 (see page 76) and arrange in a shallow kettle side by side. Add the bouillon, butter and seasoning and cook 30 minutes.

Serve hot, decorated with finely chopped parsley.

TURLU

1 lb veal
4 cups veal stock
1 cup okra
1 cup french beans (sliced)
2 cups aubergines (sliced and left in salt for 30 minutes)
2 tablespoons vinegar
6 tablespoons clarified fat

2 large onions (chopped)
3 green peppers (seeded and sliced)
1 cup marrow (diced)
1 cup tomatoes (chopped and skinned)
salt

Melt fat and fry the onions until transparent. Cut veal into small pieces, add to onions and fry for a further 20 minutes on moderate heat, stirring frequently. Remove from heat and leave aside.

Clean and prepare okra and put in a bowl with the vinegar and a generous sprinkling of salt and leave for 30 minutes, then rinse thoroughly under running water.

Put the beans and marrow in a stewpan with 2 tablespoons fat, add 2 cups stock, cover and cook 25 minutes, shaking pan occasionally.

After washing the salt and bitter juice from the aubergines, sauté them in 3 tablespoons fat for 7 minutes.

Add the okra to the beans and marrows, add meat and onions, green peppers and ½ cup of tomatoes. Add the aubergines and the rest of the tomatoes and the remaining stock and cook over moderate heat for 1¼–1½ hours.

Serve hot in own liquor.

STUFFED VINE LEAVES

ETLI YAPRAK DOLMASI

1 lb vine leaves
¼ cup rice
2 onions (chopped)
1 lb lamb mince
6 sprigs dill
½ teaspoon rosemary

1 cup white stock
1 cup white wine
½ cup sliced mushrooms
4 tablespoons clarified fat
½ teaspoon white pepper
garlic salt

Put the washed and cleaned vine leaves into boiling water and cook for 5 minutes. Strain, cut off stalks, and cut each leaf in half down the middle vein.

Melt half the fat and lightly brown the onions, add mushrooms and cook a further 3 minutes. Add the stock, the cleaned rice, and cook for 10–12 minutes on moderate heat until all liquid has been absorbed by the rice. Remove from heat, add the lamb, dill, rosemary, pepper and salt and knead for 5 minutes.

With the hairy sides of the leaves facing upwards put 1 good teaspoon of stuffing on each leaf and roll up fairly tightly, shiny sides of leaves facing outwards.

Arrange side by side at the bottom of a shallow kettle, layer by layer, and add rest of clarified fat and the wine. Cover with a plate with a heavy weight on top, put lid on kettle and cook over moderate heat for 35 minutes. Serve hot.

COLD VEGETABLE DISHES
ZEYTINYAĞLI SEBZELER

ARTICHOKE

YER ELMASI

2 lb artichokes
1 lemon
½ cup water
2 onions (chopped)
1 teaspoon garlic salt

1 cup olive oil
¼ cup rice
3 diced carrots
6 sprigs dill
½ cup sliced tomatoes (skinned)

Heat oil to boiling point, add onions and fry until transparent but not brown. Add the tomatoes and cook another 4 minutes.

Peel the artichokes thinly and slice them. Add these, with the water, to the onions, cover and cook another 15 minutes, shaking pan occasionally. Add seasoning and 3 more cups of hot water and cook until the artichokes are tender – about 15–20 minutes.

Boil rice in a separate pan, drain after 10 minutes and add the rice to the artichokes with lemon juice. Cook 3 minutes longer, uncovered, and allow to cool in own juice.

Serve very cold, garnished with the dill.

STUFFED AUBERGINE

PATLICAN DOLMASI

6 large aubergines
1 cup water
¼ cup olive oil

salt to taste
lemon and chopped parsley

Cut off stalks of aubergines and from the other end cut off a
'lid'. Scoop out insides and leave aside. Put plenty of coarse
salt in the cavities and on the outside skins and leave for
30 minutes. Wash several times under cold running water and
fill very tightly with Stuffing Number 2 (page 128). Put on
the 'lids' and arrange, upright, on a baking dish. Add water
and olive oil and salt. Cover and cook on moderate heat for
1 hour, until aubergines are soft.

Allow to cool in own liquor and serve well chilled with
thin slices of lemon and chopped parsley.

BROAD BEANS

BAKLA

2 lb fresh young beans   *1½ cups water*
½ cup olive oil   *2 bunches spring onions*
2 teaspoons sugar   *2 tablespoons chopped mint*
juice of 1 lemon   *2 tablespoons dill (chopped)*
salt to taste

String the beans and wash well. Leave them whole and pour
over them the lemon juice. Add a sprinkling of salt and leave
aside for 15 minutes. Line the bottom of a strong, broad
saucepan with a vine leaf and lay on this the biggest beans.
Pile the mint, dill and spring onions (these last should be cut
to the size of the beans) in the centre and continue filling up
with beans. Sprinkle with sugar and add water and olive oil.
Cover with greaseproof paper sprinkled with water, put on
saucepan lid and cook on a moderate heat for 1½ to 2 hours
until beans are very tender but unbroken. Do not open the
saucepan during the cooking process but shake occasionally
to prevent sticking.

Leave to get cold in the saucepan, then serve well chilled
with fresh yoğurt in which a clove of garlic has been crushed.

STUFFED CABBAGE LEAVES
LAHANA DOLMASI

1 *lb white cabbage*   *juice of* $\frac{1}{2}$ *lemon*
Pilav Stuffing 2 (see page 128)   1 *cup cold water*

Cut cabbage in half, lengthwise, and remove the tender middle part (this can be used in salads). Wash remaining cabbage and put into boiling salted water and cook for 12 minutes. Strain off water and allow to cool. Tear off the leaves gently and cut into 4-inch squares.

Put 1 good-sized teaspoon of Stuffing Number 2 on each square, fold envelope-fashion and arrange at the bottom of a shallow pan which has been lined with cabbage leaves to prevent burning.

Sprinkle on the lemon juice, add the cold water, cover with a heavy plate, put on pan lid and cook on medium heat for 1 hour. Allow to cool in own pan and serve very cold.

FRENCH BEANS IN OLIVE OIL
ZEYTINYAĞLI TAZE FASULYA

2 lb beans	¾ cup olive oil
1 large onion (finely chopped)	2 tomatoes (skinned and seeded)
1 teaspoon sugar	3 cups water
salt to taste	1 cup dry white wine

String and wash the beans and cut into long thin strips. Put
in a pan with the onions, tomatoes and salt. Add the oil and
½ cup of wine. Cover and cook about 20 minutes on medium
heat, shaking pan occasionally. Boil the rest of the wine with
all the water and add to the beans and cook, covered, until
tender. If beans are old and rather stringy and will not cook
with this amount of liquid, add a little more hot water from
time to time. Add sugar last of all, stir carefully, remove from
heat and allow to cool in pan.

Serve cold in its own liquor.

HARICOT BEANS IN OLIVE OIL
ZEYTİNYAĞLI KURU FASULYA

$\frac{3}{4}$ lb haricot beans
1 potato
2 carrots (diced)
3 cloves garlic
$\frac{1}{4}$ cup lemon juice
4 tablespoons parsley (chopped)
salt and pepper

$1\frac{1}{4}$ cups olive oil
2 sticks celery (cut small)
1 large onion (chopped)
$2\frac{3}{4}$ cups water
1 teaspoon sugar
6 spring onions

Soak beans overnight, strain, wash and put in boiling water. Cook for 30 minutes, then remove from heat.

Fry the onions in half the olive oil until pale brown, add water and bring to boil. Add celery, potato, carrots, garlic, spring onions (chopped), sugar and beans. Cover and cook on low heat until beans are tender. Add rest of oil, season and cook another 10 minutes. Add lemon juice and remove from heat.

Allow to cool in own liquor and serve cold, sprinkled with chopped parsley and crisp French bread.

AUBERGINE

IMAM BAYILDI

4 aubergines
4 large onions
12 cloves garlic
2 cups water
salt to taste

1 cup olive oil
4 tomatoes (skinned)
12 sprigs of parsley
1 teaspoon sugar

Cut the onion into thin half-moon slices. Chop the tomatoes and parsley and mix with the onion slices. Add the garlic and salt and leave aside. Leave the stalk on the aubergines but peel the dark outer skin in ½-inch wide strips lengthwise, then make a deep incision in the centre lengthwise. Sprinkle generously with coarse rock salt and leave aside for 30 minutes to extract the vegetable's bitter juices.

Wash well and pat dry. Take the onion mixture and fill the aubergines with this then lay them side by side in a wide-bottomed saucepan.

Add water, olive oil, salt and a sprinkling of sugar. Put a plate on them and then cover the saucepan. Cook until the aubergines are soft and tender and the liquor reduced to almost nothing (less than 1 tablespoon should remain in the saucepan) – about 1½ hours on medium heat. Allow to cool in own saucepan and serve very cold.

STUFFED GREEN PEPPERS

BIBER DOLMASI

6 *large green peppers*　　　　　1 *cup cold water*
Stuffing 2 (*see page* 128)

Choose the peppers of even size. Cut out the stalk carefully –
this will act as the 'lid' – and clean out all the seeds. Wash well
under running water taking care not to split the skins of the
peppers. Boil for 5 minutes, then strain this water away, add
freshly boiling water and cook another 5 minutes. Strain and
leave aside to cool.

Fill with Stuffing Number 2, adding the stalk as a 'lid'.

Stand upright in a wide shallow pan, add 1 cup of water
and cook for 50–55 minutes – at a fairly high heat to begin
with and on a medium heat for the last 5 minutes. Keep
covered throughout cooking. Leave to cool in their own
saucepan (there should be scarcely any liquor left) and serve
very cold.

STUFFED TOMATOES
DOMATES DOLMASI

6 large well shaped tomatoes $\frac{1}{2}$ *cup cold water*
Pilav Stuffing 2 (see page 128)

Wash the tomatoes and cut a lid from the top of each. Clean out insides, taking care not to break the skins. Fill with Stuffing Number 2 and arrange side by side in a shallow pan. Add the $\frac{1}{2}$ cup water, cover and cook on high heat for 5 minutes. Reduce heat and continue cooking another 45 minutes until all water has evaporated.

Leave to cool in their own pan and serve cold.

STUFFED VINE LEAVES
YAPRAK DOLMASI

1 *lb vine leaves*   *juice of ½ lemon*
1 *cup cold water*   *Pilav Stuffing 2 (see page* 128)

Put the washed and cleaned vine leaves into boiling water and cook for 5 minutes. Strain, cut off stalks, and cut each leaf in half down the middle vein. With the hairy sides of the leaves facing upwards put 1 teaspoon of Stuffing Number 2 on each leaf and roll up fairly tightly, like an envelope as far as possible, shiny sides of leaves facing outwards.

Line a shallow pan with large, washed vine leaves (this is to prevent the dolma burning) and arrange the stuffed leaves side by side. Sprinkle with the lemon juice, add the cold water, cover with a heavy plate and then the lid and cook on medium heat for 1 hour.

Allow to cool in own pan and serve cold.

BOREK AND PILAV

PILAV VE BOREKLER

BOREK WITH CHEESE

PEYNIRLI BOREK

½ lb white cheese
3 tablespoons minced parsley
1 tablespoon butter
1 egg yolk

2 mushrooms (chopped finely)
½ lb puff pastry (see 'Kebab in
    Puff Pastry', page 53)

Sauté the mushrooms in butter for 4–5 minutes, then leave aside to cool. Mix parsley, cheese and yolk of egg together and add the mushrooms.

Roll out the puff pastry very thinly, fill with the cheese mixture and cut into half-moon shapes with a pastry cutter. Seal edges with egg yolk. Grease a baking sheet and put the borek on this – 1 inch apart – glaze with beaten egg and bake in moderate oven – 350° – until golden brown, about 30 minutes.

Can be served hot or cold.

BOREK WITH CHICKEN
TAVUKLU BOREK

½–¾ lb puff pastry (see 'Kebab
  in Puff Pastry', page 53)
1 egg yolk
½ cup single cream
1 teaspoon paprika
1 teaspoon chervil (chopped)
1 breast of boiled chicken

1 tablespoon butter
½ cup milk
¼ cup flour
2 teaspoons fresh coconut
  (grated)
salt to taste

Mince the chicken breast very finely.

Melt butter, add flour and fry for 3–4 minutes, stirring all
the time. Add milk gradually, still stirring, then the cream.
Stir vigorously to prevent lumps forming. Cook for 2 minutes
until smooth and velvety. Add the breast of chicken, egg yolk,
coconut, seasoning and chervil, stir thoroughly and remove
from heat.

Roll out pastry very thinly, cut into fancy shapes and fill
with the creamed mixture. Put on a greased baking sheet,
1 inch apart, and cook until golden brown in moderate
oven – 350°.

Serve hot in a ring of green peas.

BOREK WITH LAMB

TALAS BOREK

¾ lb puff pastry (see 'Kebab in Puff Pastry', page 53)
1 lb lamb
4 onions (chopped finely)
6 sprigs chopped parsley
1 teaspoon thyme (chopped)

¼ cup white wine
2 tablespoons butter
½ tablespoon tomato ketchup
1 teaspoon pepper
1 egg
salt to taste

Cut lamb in strips, julienne fashion. Melt butter, add the meat and 1 onion and cook for 25 minutes over moderate heat. Add tomato ketchup, wine and seasoning, cover and cook over very low heat for 50 minutes. Add the rest of the onions and cook another 45 minutes until all liquid is reduced to a thick purée. During this stage shake the pan frequently to prevent sticking. Add the thyme and parsley, stir once, remove from heat and allow to cool.

Roll out the pastry very thinly, cut into 6 pieces and roll each piece until it is thin as paper. Trim into 7-inch squares and fill. Seal all edges with yolk of egg and place on a greased baking dish. Bake at 350° (moderate oven) until golden brown.

Serve hot.

BOREK WITH MINCE
KIYMALI BOREK

¾ lb puff pastry (see 'Kebab in Puff Pastry', page 53)
2 large onions (chopped finely)
½ teaspoon salt
⅛ teaspoon mace
½ mince (without fat)
1 teaspoon white pepper
½ teaspoon fresh thyme
⅛ teaspoon cinnamon

Put the mince and the onions into a saucepan, without water or fat, and on a very low heat cook for 5–7 minutes, shaking pan occasionally to prevent sticking. Add herbs and seasoning, cover and cook – still over a low heat – for about 20 minutes or until the meat has absorbed its own juice. Remove from heat and allow to get cold.

Roll out pastry thinly and cut in half. Grease an oval-shaped pie dish and shape the two pieces of pastry to fit it. Line the dish with pastry, add the filling and cover with the rest of the pastry. Prick a few holes here and there so that the steam can escape and brush top generously with beaten egg. Cook in a hot oven (400°) for about 35 minutes or until the top is golden brown.

CHICKEN PILAV

TAVUKLU PILAV

1 *boiled chicken* (2 *lb*)
2 *tablespoons flour*
1 *lb rice* (*Patna*)
½ *cup single cream*

2 *cups chicken stock*
3 *tablespoons grated parmesan*
4 *tablespoons butter*
salt and white pepper

Separate legs and breast of chicken and cut rest into very small pieces. Make pilav with 1½ cups of the chicken stock but before adding the rice to the boiling stock put in the pieces of cut-up chicken – bring to boiling point again and then put in the rice. Now proceed as for the making of plain pilav (page 126).

In a separate pan melt 1 tablespoon butter, add flour and cook for 3 minutes, stirring all the time. Add the remaining ½ cup of chicken stock, stir, add cream gradually and stir until smooth and creamy – about 5 minutes. Remove from heat, add 1 more tablespoon butter, stir and keep hot beside the fire.

Serve the pilav, arrange the legs and slices of breast of chicken around the dish, pour on the cream sauce and sprinkle with the grated Parmesan.

Serve immediately.

PILAV WITH LAMB
KUZULU PILAV

1 lb lamb
1½ cups white stock
1 teaspoon white pepper
1 onion (chopped)
1 teaspoon cinnamon
4 tablespoons butter
1 tablespoon currants
1 tomato (skinned and chopped)
3 sprigs parsley

1 cup Patna rice
1 tablespoon pine kernels
1 teaspoon sugar
1 tablespoon dill
¼ cup clarified fat
½ lb lamb's liver
½ teaspoon mignonette salt
3 spring onions
1 leaf rosemary

Put the lamb and clarified fat in a baking tin and roast in moderate oven until nicely browned, basting every 10 minutes. Remove when cooked and keep in a warm place.

Clean liver and cut in very small pieces, sauté for 3 minutes in 2 tablespoons butter, then leave aside to keep warm. Cut up spring onions and sauté in same butter for 2 minutes and leave aside to keep warm.

Clean and prepare rice as for plain pilav (page 126). Melt remaining butter and fry onions until beginning to brown slightly. Add pine kernels and cook until these are golden brown – be careful onions do not burn during this time. Add rice and fry another 5 minutes. Add pepper, salt, cleaned currants, sugar, spring onions, herbs, tomatoes and stock. Stir once, cover and cook 5 minutes on high heat then reduce flame to very low and cook until all liquid has been absorbed by the rice – about 6 minutes more, although if rice is old it may take a minute or so longer. Add the liver and the minced parsley, stir with a wooden spoon, add spring onions, cover with a napkin and put on lid. Leave to 'rest' for 40 minutes as near fire as possible. Stir once more then serve with slices of roast lamb on top garnished with cinnamon.

PLAIN PILAV

PILAV

1 *cup Patna rice*	1¾ *cups white stock*
2 *tablespoons butter*	½ *teaspoon salt*

Clean rice, lay on a shallow dish and pour boiling water over it. Leave until the water is quite cold, strain and wash several times under running cold water.

Melt butter in a large pan, heat but do not allow to burn. Add stock and salt and bring to boil quickly. Add the drained rice and cook at the same temperature for 5 minutes, then turn heat to very, very low and cook until all stock has been absorbed – 7–8 minutes – when there should be holes all over the rice. Test with a wooden spoon and if this stands upright then the rice is cooked.

Remove from heat, take off lid, put a napkin over saucepan then replace the lid again. Leave close to the fire to keep hot for 30–35 minutes – this 'resting' period is the most important part of pilav making.

Remove lid and napkin, stir well with a wooden spoon until each grain stands separately and serve at once.

SHRIMP PILAV WITH SAFFRON
TEKE VE SAFRONLI PILAV

1 *cup Patna rice*
2 *tablespoons butter*
1 *carrot (diced)*
1 *clove of garlic (mashed)*
3 *peppercorns*
2½ *cups water*

1 *cup cooked shrimps*
2 *stalks celery (cut small)*
1 *large onion (chopped)*
½ *teaspoon salt*
1 *teaspoon basil*
½ *teaspoon saffron*

Heat the butter and fry in it the onions, garlic, celery and carrot, until the onions are a golden brown. Add half the shrimps, the peppercorns and all the herbs and cook another 3–4 minutes. Add the water and cook another 15 minutes. Remove peppercorns and pass the rest of the mixture through a sieve. Dissolve saffron in a very little hot water then pour into the liquid through muslin.

From this liquid measure out 1½ cups, add ½ tablespoon butter, allow to melt then add the washed and cleaned rice. After 2 minutes' cooking turn heat to very low and cook for 15 minutes, when all the liquid should have been absorbed by the rice. Put the rest of the shrimps on top of the rice, cover again and leave beside the fire to 'rest' for 40 minutes with a napkin under the lid to absorb the excess moisture.

Stir once to separate the grains and serve immediately.

STUFFING FOR GREEN PEPPERS, TOMATOES, VINE LEAVES ETC: II

1 cup rice
½ cup water
5 large onions (chopped
   finely)
1 tablespoon pine kernels
1 teaspoon sugar
1 teaspoon mixed herbs
sprig of mint (chopped)

1 cup olive oil
½ cup cider
1 large tomato (skinned)
1 tablespoon currants
1 teaspoon pepper
sprig of dill (chopped)
mignonette salt

Clean and cover rice with hot water and leave aside until water is cold. Wash several times under running water, strain and leave aside.

Fry onions in oil for 10 minutes. Add rice and pine kernels, cover pan and cook for 20 minutes on moderate heat, stirring occasionally to avoid sticking. Add the chopped tomato, currants, dill, mint, mixed herbs, water and cider, stir and cook for another 15 minutes. Add sugar last of all and use the stuffing as directed in the recipes.

NOTE: *This stuffing must only be used in dishes which are to be served cold.*

DESSERTS
TATLILAR

ALMOND CREAM WITH SHERRY SAUCE
ŞARAPLI KREMLI BADEM

¼ *cup butter*
¼ *cup ground sweet almonds*
4 *large egg yolks*
¼ *cup caster sugar*

¼ *cup grated chocolate*
  (unsweetened)
4 *egg whites*

Brush a tube mould with almond oil.

Cream the butter and sugar until white and fluffy then beat in the egg yolks, one at a time, and continue beating for 2 minutes.

Whisk egg whites until they hold a peak, then fold gently into the mixture.

Add ground almonds and chocolate and stir once, thoroughly but quickly. Pour mixture into the mould and steam over hot water for 45 minutes.

SHERRY SAUCE:

½ *cup sugar*
1 *cup dark sherry*

½ *cup grated chocolate*
  (unsweetened)

Put sugar, salt, chocolate and sherry into a pan and cook until thick, stirring all the time.

When the almond cream is unmoulded pour the hot sauce over it – first having filled the centre of the mould with vanilla ice cream.

ALMOND FINGERS

BADEM TATLISI

¾ cup ground sweet almonds
6 large eggs
4 cups sugar
3 cups fresh peach juice
halved fresh peaches

1 cup flour
2 tablespoons butter
⅛ teaspoon salt
½ cup pralined almonds

Grease and flour a 9-inch square tin.

Separate egg yolks, add ¾ cup sugar and beat for 6–7 minutes.

Add salt to egg whites and beat until stiff and glossy, then fold carefully into the yolks. Add the almonds and flour and the melted butter. Stir quickly and pour into the greased tin. Bake 50 minutes in a moderate oven – 350°.

Put the peach juice and remaining sugar (3¼ cups) into a saucepan and boil for 15 minutes uncovered, stirring until all sugar has been dissolved. Pour this syrup over the almond sweet (it should be left in tin until cold) and leave aside overnight if possible.

Cut into fingers and serve with the halved peaches and pralined almonds.

NOTE: To praline almonds: Chop some almonds and brown them very evenly in the oven, sprinkling them frequently with icing sugar. The heat of the oven causes the sugar to caramelise on the almonds.

ALMOND TART WITH CARAMEL SAUCE

KAREMELA SALÇALI BADEM TATLISI

6 egg yolks
1 teaspoon baking powder
1 teaspoon salt
½ teaspoon cream of tartar
¾ cup sugar
Whipped cream filling
  (almond flavour)

¾ cup flour (4 times sifted)
¼ cup sugar
6 egg whites
¾ cup toasted almonds (finely
  chopped)
½ cup hot water
caramel sauce

Caramelise the ¾ cup sugar by melting it in a heavy saucepan over a low heat, stirring continuously until brown. Add the hot water and stir until the mixture is very smooth and creamy.

Beat egg yolks until thick and lemon coloured and stir in two tablespoons of the slightly cooled caramel mixture. Sift together the flour, baking powder and salt and stir into the egg yolks.

Beat the egg whites and cream of tartar together until the mixture holds a peak, then beat in gradually the ¼ cup of sugar and go on beating until very stiff and glossy. Fold in the toasted almonds and last of all fold in the egg yolk mixture.

Line two 9-inch layer pans with greased paper, brushed over with a little warm almond oil, and pour in the mixture. Bake in a moderate oven, 350°, for about 30 minutes or until, when touched gently with the finger, no imprint remains.

Turn out of pans, remove paper and cool. Put together with almond flavoured whipped cream filling and cover with caramel sauce – which is made as follows. Add to the caramelised sugar left in the heavy saucepan:

½ cup sugar
¼ teaspoon salt
¼ cup single cream

¼ cup butter
½ cup single cream

Stir all together until smooth and cook over a moderate heat, stirring now and then until the mixture reaches 234°. Now add the ¼ cup of cream and cook again to 234°. Remove from heat. When partly cooled (do not stir during this time) pour over the top and sides of the tart. Serve cold.

TO MAKE WHIPPED CREAM FILLING:

½ teaspoon gelatin
1 cup double cream
1 teaspoon almond essence

1 tablespoon single cream
¼ cup sifted icing sugar

Soften the gelatin in the single cream, dissolve over a pan of hot water. Whip the double cream until stiff, beat in the icing sugar, the cooled gelatin and the almond flavouring. Chill slightly before use.

APRICOT MERINGUE

KAYISI

2 cups fresh apricots
1 cup ground sweet almonds
1 cup whipped cream
¾ teaspoon cream of tartar
3–4 tablespoons dark sherry

1½ cups sugar
½ cup pine kernels
3 egg whites
1 tablespoon lemon juice

Put the stoned apricots and lemon juice into a saucepan and cook on a low heat until plenty of liquid has been extracted from the fruit. Add 1 cup sugar, stir until dissolved, cover and cook for 30 minutes over low heat. Remove from heat and cool.

Mix ½ cup each of ground almonds, sugar and pine kernels with enough sherry to make a softish paste. Fill the apricots with this mixture. Arrange in a greased glass oven dish, sprinkling the rest of the ground almonds over them and adding their own syrup.

Beat the egg whites with the cream of tartar until stiff and glossy and spread over the whole, taking special care that the meringue reaches right to the sides of the dish and the apricots are not exposed in any place. Bake in a coolish oven – 300° – until meringue is firm and set and delicately browned.

Serve hot.

ASHUREY

AŞURE

¼ lb wheat (whole wheat)
1 cup sugar
¼ cup haricot beans (cooked)
¼ cup Spanish nohut
½ cup dates
½ cup figs
½ cup blanched almonds (halved)
½ cup rosewater

2 cups milk
¼ cup rice
¼ cup butter beans (cooked)
¼ cup currants
½ cup sultanas
½ cup chopped walnuts
¼ cup pine kernels

The haricot and butter beans should be soaked overnight, then cooked until soft but unbroken, drained and left to cool.

Cook the wheat and rice in separate saucepans in plenty of water until very tender. Strain, keeping water in which they were cooked, and put through a sieve.

Using 5 cups of the water used for cooking rice and wheat, add the milk and sugar and bring to boil, stirring until sugar is dissolved. Boil until it thickens – a few minutes – then add the beans and Spanish nohut and all other ingredients. Boil for a further 2–3 minutes.

Serve cold in individual cups decorated with sultanas, whole walnuts and pomegranate drenched in icing sugar.

BAKLAVA WITH WALNUTS

BAKLAVA

baklava pastry (this is
   obtainable at the Oriental
   Stores in Soho)
½ cup butter

1 *cup water*
1 *cup finely chopped walnuts*
1½ *cups sugar*
1 *tablespoon lemon juice*

Making baklava pastry is an art and it cannot be made at home. Even in the Middle East, where the women spend most of their time in the kitchen, baklava pastry is bought from the market. There are many recipes for the home-made product but baklava made with them never achieves the same lightness as the market product.

Grease and flour a shallow 9-inch square pan.

Roll out the baklava pastry very carefully to avoid breaking and cut into 8 pieces which should fit the pan exactly.

Take 4 pieces of the pastry and brush each *thoroughly* with melted butter and lay them in the tin one on top of the other. Cover the fourth layer with chopped walnuts. Place the other 4 pieces of pastry on top of the first four (again each layer brushed thoroughly with the melted butter) and if there is any butter left pour it all on the top layer. With a very sharp knife cut right through the 8 layers in diamond shapes. Bake in a moderate oven until nicely browned – about 65 minutes.

Put the sugar, water and lemon juice in a pan and boil for 15 minutes, stirring until sugar is dissolved. Cool a little.

When the baklava is taken from the oven, brush the whole top with butter and leave for 10 minutes. Pour the syrup into the tin and allow to cool. Serve after 24 hours' rest.

BAKLAVA WITH GROUND ALMONDS
BADEMLI BAKLAVA

baklava pastry   *2 cups ground sweet almonds*
1½ cups butter   *1½ cups sugar*
1 cup fresh apricot juice   *½ tablespoon lemon juice*
halved fresh apricots

Grease a shallow 9-inch square tray.

Use pastry as in previous recipe and cut into 8 pieces the size of the tray.

Line the pan with 1 piece of the pastry, brush thoroughly over every part with melted butter and spread evenly with ground almonds. Continue like this until the 8 pieces of pastry have been used, finishing off with a layer of plain pastry. Use up any left-over butter on this. Cut with a very sharp knife through the 8 pieces – in squares – and bake in a moderate oven until brown – about 65 minutes.

Make a syrup with the apricot juice, lemon juice and sugar and boil for 15 minutes.

Brush the cooked baklava with butter and leave for 10 minutes then pour over them the warm syrup.

Leave for 24 hours before serving with halved fresh apricots rolled in icing sugar.

BLACKCURRANT SPONGE
KUŞ UZUMU TATLISI

1 tablespoon gelatin

1 cup hot blackcurrant juice

2 tablespoons lemon juice

¼ cup fresh blackcurrants

¼ cup cold water

¾ cup brown sugar

2 egg whites

1 cup whipped cream

Soften the gelatin in the cold water. Stir in the hot juice, lemon juice, and sugar and stir until all the sugar has dissolved. Strain and cool, stirring now and then. When partly set, beat with a rotary beater until frothy. Beat the egg whites until they hold a point and fold in, then beat again with the rotary beater until all the mixture is stiff and holds a point.

Pile into tall sherbet glasses, chill for several hours and serve with whipped cream and fresh blackcurrants.

CHICKEN BREASTS
TAVUK GOGSU

$\frac{1}{2}$ a chicken breast (uncooked)
1 cup single cream
2 tablespoons cornflour
$\frac{1}{8}$ teaspoon salt
enough white wine to cover
   breast when cooking

3 cups milk
1 cup sugar
3 tablespoons ground rice
1 teaspoon ground cinnamon
crystallised violets

Cook the chicken breast in the wine slowly, removing from heat a few minutes before thoroughly cooked. Strain off wine and shred the breast finely (preferably in a machine). Put the shreds into boiling water to cleanse away all fatty residue and wash well. Repeat this process several times with fresh hot water, then dry and leave aside. Put the milk, cream, salt and sugar in a saucepan and bring to boil, stirring frequently to prevent cream from sticking. Mix the cornflour and ground rice with a little cold water and add to boiling milk and cook until mixture is of a fairly thick consistency, stirring continuously. Add the shredded chicken breast and cook another 7–8 minutes. Pour into individual moulds, wetted, and chill thoroughly.

Unmould, sprinkle with cinnamon and decorate with the crystallised violets.

NOTE: The wine in which the breast was stewed can be used in soups or stocks, etc.

CHOCOLATE MARSHMALLOW

ÇIKOLATA TATLISI

1 *tablespoon gelatin*
2 *cups milk*
2 *oz unsweetened chocolate*
¼ *cup ground sweet almonds*
1 *cup whipped cream*

¼ *cup milk*
½ *cup sugar*
¼ *lb cut up marshmallows*
3 *egg whites*
slivers of milk chocolate

Dissolve the gelatin in the ¼ cup milk.

Put 2 cups of milk, sugar and unsweetened chocolate into a saucepan and heat. Beat very fast for 2 minutes, then remove from heat. Add gelatin and milk and continue beating until smooth and creamy. Remove from heat, chill until it begins to set.

Stir in the marshmallows and the almonds and fold in the egg whites, stiffly beaten. Fold in whipped cream and chill thoroughly.

Serve in tall sherbet glasses decorated with the slivers of milk chocolate.

FRUIT COMPÔTE

MEYVA KOMPOSTOSU

1 cup strawberries
1 cup green grapes (seedless)
1½ tablespoons gelatin
1½ cups unsweetened grape
  juice (hot)
⅛ teaspoon salt
1 teaspoon grated lemon rind
whipped cream
  (Cointreau flavoured)

1 cup black cherries (stoned)
1 cup halved fresh peaches
¼ cup cold water
¾ cup caster sugar
1 teaspoon lemon juice
⅓ cup Cointreau

Soften the gelatin in cold water, stir in the hot grape juice, sugar and salt. Stir until the sugar and gelatin are completely dissolved. Cool. Stir in the lemon juice and rind and chill until beginning to set. Add Cointreau and whisk well. Add the fruits and pour into an oiled mould. Chill until set.

Unmould and serve with whipped cream.

GROUND RICE PUDDING

MUHALLEBI

3 *cups milk*
¾ *cup caster sugar*
3 *tablespoons ground rice*
⅛ *teaspoon salt*
a little icing sugar

1 *cup single cream*
1½ *tablespoons cornflour*
½ *cup ground sweet almonds*
½ *cup rosewater* (*triple strength*)
crystallised roses for garnish

Boil milk and cream with the sugar and salt.

Mix cornflour and ground rice with a little water and add this slowly to the boiling milk, stirring continuously. Cook until the mixture becomes a thickish custard (stirring all the time as this sweet burns easily). Add ground almonds, stir and remove from heat.

Pour into individual moulds (wetted) and chill.

Unmould, sprinkle each with rosewater and a little icing sugar and decorate with the roses.

HELVA

1 cup fine semolina
1 cup milk
½ cup butter
½ teaspoon vanilla

1 cup sugar
1 cup single cream
¼ cup blanched almonds
   (halved)

Melt butter and add the almonds and cook for 2 minutes. Add the semolina and continue cooking over a gentle heat for 40 minutes, stirring continuously.

In a saucepan boil the milk and the cream and add sugar. Remove from heat and add vanilla.

Add the milk and cream to the semolina mixture, stir well, cover and leave beside the fire for 15–20 minutes.

Serve when only slightly warm.

NOTE: The time of 40 minutes given above for the cooking of the semolina is correct only if the correct heat is used – it may take a few minutes longer or less – but the surest guide is when the almonds have browned considerably and a definite almond smell comes from the mixture.

KADINGOBEĞI

2 cups sifted flour

2 cups sugar

1½ cups water

3 eggs

1 cup butter

3 tablespoons butter

2 cups water

½ tablespoon lemon juice

⅛ teaspoon salt

½ cup whipped cream

Put the sugar, lemon juice and the 2 cups of water in a saucepan, boil for 15 minutes then leave aside to cool.

Melt butter and when sizzling add salt and the rest of the water (1½ cups). Bring to boil and add the flour. Cook for 5 minutes, stirring all the time. Remove from heat and when cold add the eggs and knead for 7–8 minutes. Take pieces of the dough, about the size of a walnut, and shape into balls. Flatten and make a hole through the centre with your finger, grease round the hole with a very little almond oil.

Melt butter and fry the balls – at first on a very low heat until they start to swell when the heat should be slightly raised. Cook on both sides until a deep golden brown. Toss each one into the syrup, leave 5 minutes and serve cold with the whipped cream.

Always remember to cool off the butter before starting to cook another batch and to increase the heat only when the balls begin swelling.

KESHKUL

1 *cup sugar*	2 *cups milk*
2 *cups single cream*	2 *tablespoons ground rice*
1 *cup ground sweet almonds*	½ *cup grated fresh coconut*
½ *cup pomegranate*	⅛ *teaspoon salt*
¼ *cup pine kernels*	1 *cup clotted cream*

Pour 1 cup scalded cream over ½ cup of the ground almonds, stir well, pass through a sieve and then put aside.

Boil the rest of the cream with the milk, add salt, and stir frequently as cream sticks very quickly. Mix the ground rice with a little milk and pour into the saucepan. Boil gently for 5 minutes, stirring all the time. Add sugar and the sieved cream and almond mixture and boil until thick. Remove from heat and pour into a wetted tube mould. Chill several hours.

Unmould and fill centre with the rest of the ground almonds, mixed with the grated coconut and pine kernels and top with the pomegranate.

Sprinkle with icing sugar and finish off with clotted cream.

LMOND PUDDING
(Keshkul)

akes 4 servings (about ¾ cup each)
ictured on page 27)

cups half-and-half
½ cups milk
cup ground almonds
cup sugar
teaspoon almond extract
teaspoon vanilla
cup milk
cup rice flour
Chopped almonds, if desired
Unsalted pistachios, if desired

1. Heat half-and-half, 1½ cups milk, the ground almonds, sugar, almond extract and vanilla in 2-quart saucepan over medium heat, stirring frequently, to boiling; remove from heat. Cover; let stand 20 minutes.

2. Strain mixture; discard almonds. Stir ½ cup milk into the rice flour in small bowl until smooth. Heat strained mixture and rice flour mixture in 2-quart saucepan over low heat, stirring constantly, until mixture coats spoon, about 10 minutes. Cool slightly; pour into individual serving dishes. Refrigerate covered until set, about 3 hours. Sprinkle with almonds and pistachios.

LEMON PUDDING
LIMONLU KREMA

¼ cup sifted flour	I cup caster sugar
¼ teaspoon salt	rind of I lemon, grated
⅓ cup lemon juice	3 large egg yolks
I cup single cream	3 egg whites
1½ cups lemon jelly	I cup vanilla ice cream

Sift together the flour, sugar and salt. Stir in the lemon rind and juice. Beat the egg yolks until thick and creamy, stir in to mixture and add cream.

Beat the egg whites until stiff and holding a peak, then fold in. Pour into a ring mould, oiled, set in a pan of water and bake in moderate oven – 350° – for 55–60 minutes.

Allow to cool thoroughly.

After unmoulding, fill the centre of the ring with chopped lemon jelly and serve with vanilla ice cream.

LEMON JELLY
JELATINLI LIMON

1½ tablespoons gelatin	I cup hot water
¼ cup lemon juice	¼ cup dry white wine (hot)
rind of I lemon	½ cup caster sugar

Dissolve the gelatin in the lemon juice, add sugar, hot water and lemon rind and stir until the sugar has dissolved. Strain through muslin, add the hot wine and pour into a wetted mould. Leave to set.

LOKMA

1 lb flour
1 tablespoon yeast
1 tablespoon butter
1¼ cups white wine
½ cup whipped cream

1 cup soft butter
1½ cups sugar
½ teaspoon salt
¾ cup water
½ cup fresh pineapple slices

Put the wine and sugar into a saucepan and when the sugar has dissolved bring to the boil, stirring all the time, and boil rapidly without a lid for 15 minutes. Remove from heat and allow to cool.

Sieve the flour 3 times, add the yeast – dissolved in 1 tablespoon water – the tablespoon of butter and the salt. Add the ¾ cup of water slowly and mix into a thick batter. Leave in a warm place to rise for 1 hour. Punch down, cover and leave to rise again for a further 1 hour. Now put the batter through a forcing bag and pipe pieces the size of a walnut into the cup of butter which should by this time be very hot. Fry until pale brown and remove from heat. After 15 minutes has elapsed return the pieces again to the hot butter and cook until deep golden brown. Toss into the cooled syrup, leave 5 minutes then remove to a serving dish.

Serve cold with the whipped cream and pineapple slices.

PLUM DESSERTS

ERIK TATLISI

2 cups large black plums
1¼ cups sifted flour
2 teaspoons caster sugar
⅓ cup ground sweet almonds
½–¾ cup butter
chopped pistachio nuts
½ cup Marsala

2 egg whites
1½ teaspoons grated lemon rind
a little rosewater (about 3 tablespoons)
icing sugar
½ cup whipped cream

Wash the plums and stone them. Do this with a long needle, taking care not to break the outer skin. Fill with ground sweet almonds sprinkled with a little rosewater.

Whisk the Marsala, flour, lemon rind and sugar together to make a sort of batter and leave aside for 1 hour. Whisk again and fold in the stiffly beaten egg whites.

Melt the butter, coat the plums in the wine batter, and fry until a golden brown (the batter should puff up considerably).

Drain and roll in icing sugar and pistachio nuts. Serve hot with a little whipped cream piped over each.

RASPBERRY SHORTCAKE

FRAMBUVAZ KURABIYESI

2 cups sifted flour (plain
   flour)
2½ teaspoons baking powder
6 tablespoons soft butter
3 cups raspberries
3 tablespoons port wine
3 tablespoons flour

2 cups water
3 tablespoons caster sugar
1 teaspoon salt
⅔ cup milk
½ cup caster sugar
¼ cup soft butter
1½ cups sugar

Marinate the raspberries, port wine and ½ cup caster sugar for 1 hour, turning the fruit now and then.

Put the 1½ cups sugar and the 2 cups water in an oblong baking pan and boil for 6 minutes, stirring all the time.

Sift together the flour, 3 tablespoons caster sugar, baking powder and salt, blend in the 6 tablespoons of softened butter, then stir in the milk. Knead lightly and roll out to ⅓ inch thickness into an oblong shape 6 inches × 12 inches.

Spread this with the marinated raspberries (the liquid as well).

Mix the ¼ cup soft butter and the 3 tablespoons flour and spread over the fruit. Roll up lengthwise, seal the edges carefully and place the roll in the hot syrup in the baking pan.

Bake for 35–40 minutes at 450°, basting with the syrup from time to time.

Serve cold cut in thick slices with whole raspberries and unsweetened whipped cream.

REVANI

1 *cup fine semolina*
8 *eggs*
2 *tablespoons flour*
2 *teaspoons lemon rind*
1 *cup clotted cream*

4 *cups sugar*
2 *tablespoons butter*
3 *cups Marsala*
⅛ *teaspoon salt*

Grease and flour a 9-inch square tin.

Separate yolks of eggs, add 1 cup of the sugar and the lemon rind and beat for 7–8 minutes.

Beat the whites with the salt until holding a peak and fold into the yolks. Add the sifted flour and the semolina, stir very carefully then pour in the butter which should have been melted. Pour into the greased tin and cook at 350° (moderate oven) until delicately browned – about 1 hour.

Put the Marsala and the remaining 3 cups of sugar into a saucepan, bring to the boil slowly, stirring until all sugar has been dissolved. Boil rapidly for 15 minutes, uncovered.

Pour the hot syrup over the revani, in the tin in which it was cooked, and leave to cool.

Serve after 24 hours with clotted cream.

RICE IN WINE SYRUP
SUTLAÇ ŞARAPLI

½ cup rice
1 cup single cream
2 tablespoons butter
⅛ teaspoon salt
¼ cup ground sweet almonds
¾ cup sugar

1 cup milk
3 tablespoons caster sugar
2 large eggs
¼ cup seedless raisins
1 cup whipped cream
⅓ cup red or white wine

Clean the rice and boil it in plenty of water until soft. Strain off any surplus water and add the milk, cream, butter, raisins, caster sugar and salt. Cook until mixture is very thick, stirring frequently to prevent sticking. Remove from heat and allow to get cold.

Add the beaten eggs and the almonds and stir well. Pour the whole into a greased baking dish and bake until top is golden brown in a moderate oven – 350°. Remove from oven, cut into triangular shapes in the baking dish and leave to cool.

Put the ¾ cup of sugar and the wine into a saucepan and boil until a thickish syrup is obtained – about 10 minutes fast boiling – stirring until all sugar has been dissolved.

Pour this over the rice shapes and serve cold – any syrup not absorbed by rice can be poured over – with whipped cream.

STRAWBERRY CREAM PUFFS

ÇILEKLI PASTALAR

1 *cup water*
1 *cup sifted flour*
1 *cup double cream*
1 *cup cut up strawberries*

½ *cup butter*
4 *large eggs*
½ *cup icing sugar*

Heat the water and the butter to boiling point. Add the flour
and stir constantly until the mixture leaves the sides of the pan
and forms a ball (about 1½–2 minutes).

Remove from heat and cool.

Beat in the eggs one by one and continue beating until the
mixture is smooth and velvety. Drop the mixture from a
large spoon on an ungreased baking tray – at least 3 inches
apart – and bake at 400° for about 45 minutes or until they
are puffed, dry and golden brown. Cool slowly in a warm,
draught-free place.

Cut off tops with a sharp knife and scoop out any soft inside
dough. Whip the cream until very stiff, add icing sugar and
beat again. Fold in the cut-up strawberries and fill the puffs
with this mixture. Replace the tops and dust with icing sugar.
Serve cold.

TULUMBA TATLISI

2 *tablespoons butter*	*bananas cut lengthwise*
1 *tablespoon ground rice*	1 *cup flour*
3 *large eggs*	½ *tablespoon arrowroot*
1 *cup olive oil*	⅛ *teaspoon salt*
1 *cup grape juice (white grapes)*	1½ *cups sugar*
	½ *cup white wine*

Boil the sugar and grape juice for 15 minutes until a thickish syrup has formed, then remove from heat and put aside.

Melt the butter and add the wine and salt. Bring to boiling point slowly. Add very gradually the twice sifted flour and cook over a low heat for 8 minutes, stirring all the time. Remove from heat and add the ground rice and arrowroot (previously mixed with a little water). Leave to cool.

When almost cold add the eggs and knead for 8 minutes, then put through a forcing bag with a third-inch wide nozzle.

Heat olive oil a little and pipe 2-inch lengths of the mixture into it. Cook on a low heat until they begin to swell, then increase the heat and cook until golden brown on both sides. (If more than one batch has to be cooked, always cool off the olive oil before piping the fresh mixture into it and never increase heat until swelling has started.) Toss the tulumba in the syrup, leave 5 minutes and serve cold on the sliced bananas.

TURKISH DELIGHT

LOKUM

4 *cups sugar*
4 *tablespoons cornflour*
1 *teaspoon almond oil*
2 *teaspoons rosewater*
a few drops of cochineal
2 *cups water*

1 *teaspoon cream of tartar*
1 *cup icing sugar*
1 *tablespoon finely chopped
pistachio nuts*
6 *tablespoons grape juice
(white grape)*

Boil sugar and water for 20 minutes, stirring until sugar is dissolved. Mix cornflour with grape juice and add this, gradually, to the syrup, stirring all the time. Add the cream of tartar and continue stirring. Boil until mixture is thick and no smell of cornflour comes from it, then remove from heat. Add rosewater and cochineal and pour into a long shallow tray *well brushed* with almond oil and leave until cold. With a sharp knife cut into squares, roll in icing sugar and serve.

The sweets can also be rolled in a mixture of half icing sugar, half coconut.

s

~~

ikle
ure. Fold
ter. for m-

A   o s
s   e:

reʃ

TURKISH COFFEE

KAHVE

To each *small* coffee cup use 2 teaspoons Turkish coffee (this is the fine, powdered coffee, as fine as cocoa) and from 1–2 teaspoons sugar, depending upon how sweet you like it.

A brass, copper-lined cezva with a long handle is the correct implement for cooking it, preferably over a charcoal fire. But a small saucepan may be used quite successfully.

For three people use:

    3 coffee cups water (the smallest coffee cups)
    3–6 heaped teaspoons sugar
    6 rounded teaspoons Turkish coffee

Put water (cold), sugar and coffee into the saucepan and over a very low heat (this is most important), bring to the boil, stirring at first until all the sugar has been dissolved. Allow to come barely to the boil, to froth up, then remove from flame and allow the froth to subside. Repeat this three times, allow to subside and serve immediately, pouring a little into each cup at first so that the brown froth is distributed evenly.

Incidentally, never wash the saucepan too thoroughly. Keep one saucepan for the making of Turkish coffee and never do more than rinse it out in cold water. In this way the saucepan becomes well and truly 'seasoned' and your coffee flavour improves.

INDEX

SHREDDED WHEAT PASTRY
(Tel Kadayif)
Makes 12 to 14 servings

1   package (10 ounces) shredded wheat
     biscuits
½   cup butter or margarine, melted
1   cup ground walnuts

¼   cup sugar
½   cup butter or margarine, melted
     Milk Syrup (recipe follows)
     Heat oven to 400°

1. Dip half the wheat biscuits quickly in
to hot water one at a time. Split biscuit
along seam with fork; arrange in greas
13 x 9 x 2-inch baking pan. Spoon ½ cu
butter over biscuits. Bake until golden
about 15 minutes.

2. Sprinkle walnuts and sugar over h
biscuits. Dip remaining biscuits quickly
into hot water one at a time. Split biscuits along seam with fork; arrange on
top of walnuts. Spoon ½ cup butter over
biscuits. Bake until golden and crisp,
about 30 minutes.

3. Make Milk Syrup.

4. Spoon hot Milk Syrup over pastry.
Cool completely. Allow all of the Milk
Syrup to absorb, about 8 hours. Cut into
squares.

MILK SYRUP

1½ cups milk
1⅓ cups sugar

Heat milk and sugar in 2-quart saucepan over medium heat, stirring constantly, to boiling; remove from heat.   ○

SPINACH SALAD
(Borani)
Makes 8 servings (pictured on page 24)

2   quarts spinach, washed, trimmed
1   small red onion, thinly sliced

2   oranges, peeled, cut into 1-inch pieces
1   cup yogurt (see recipe, page 38)
3   tablespoons olive oil
1   tablespoon lemon juice
1   teaspoon sugar
½   teaspoon celery seeds
½   teaspoon salt
¼   teaspoon freshly ground pepper

Combine spinach and onion in 2-quart
glass bowl. Arrange oranges on spinach
Place remaining ingredients in jar with
tight-fitting lid; cover and shake. Pour
into center of salad. Toss just before
serving.

SWEET COOKIES
(Sekerpare)

Makes about 2½ dozen (pictured on page 27)

- 1 cup butter or margarine
- 1 cup powdered sugar
- 3 eggs
- 3½ cups all-purpose flour
- 1 tablespoon baking powder
- ¼ teaspoon salt
- Syrup (recipe follows)
- Unblanched whole almonds
- 1 egg yolk, beaten

1. Cream butter and sugar until light and fluffy. Add 3 eggs; beat well. Stir in flour, baking powder and salt until stiff. Refrigerate covered 1 hour.

2. Make Syrup.

3. Heat oven to 350°. Shape dough into 1½-inch balls. Place balls on greased baking sheets 2 inches apart. Dip almonds into beaten egg yolk. Press an almond into each ball. Brush each ball with Syrup. Bake until golden, 20 to 25 minutes; remove from baking sheet. Dip each cookie into remaining Syrup; cool on wire rack.

SYRUP

- 1½ cups sugar
- 1 cup water
- 1 teaspoon lemon juice

Heat all ingredients in 2-quart saucepan over medium heat, stirring occasionally, to boiling; reduce heat. Simmer uncovered, stirring occasionally, 10 minutes.

TURKISH PILAF
(Nancy Ofiara, Melbourne, Fla.)

Preparation time: 30 minutes.
Makes 2 servings.*

- ¾ cup long-grain rice
- 2 tablespoons instant beef broth
- 4 teaspoons ground cinnamon
- ½ cup pitted prunes, chopped
- ¼ cup golden raisins
- ¾ pound lean ground lamb or beef
- 1 large onion, sliced
- 1 tablespoon butter
- 1 teaspoon freshly ground black pepper
- ¼ teaspoon curry powder
- 3 tablespoons fresh lemon juice
- 3 tablespoons fresh minced parsley
- ½ cup slivered almonds, lightly browned in 4 tablespoons butter
- ½ teaspoon salt
- ¼ teaspoon pepper

1. Cook rice following label directions but adding 1 tablespoon of the broth, 1 teaspoon of the cinnamon, the prunes and raisins with the rice.

2. Sauté lamb and onion in butter in a large skillet just until no pink remains. Stir in pepper, curry powder, remaining tablespoon broth and cinnamon; cook 2 minutes longer. Add rice mixture to meat. Stir in lemon juice, 2 tablespoons of the parsley and ¼ cup of the almonds with butter. Cover; simmer 5 minutes. Taste; add additional salt and pepper, if needed. Garnish with remaining parsley and almonds.

*Double ingredients for 4 servings.

SESAME RINGS
(Simit)
Makes about 2 dozen

1   cup yogurt (see recipe, page 38)
¾   cup safflower oil
¼   cup olive oil
1   teaspoon baking soda
1   teaspoon salt
4   cups all-purpose flour
1   egg, beaten
½   cup sesame seeds
    Heat oven to 400°

1. Combine yogurt and oils in large bowl. Stir in baking soda and salt. Stir in flour to make stiff dough (knead with hands if necessary).

2. Shape a tablespoon of dough into a 6-inch rope. Shape rope into ring about 2 inches in diameter. Repeat with remaining dough. Dip rings in beaten egg, then dip in sesame seeds. Bake on well-greased baking sheets until brown, about 20 minutes.

Su with chicken Yogurt Soup

TIP: Sesame Rings can be made up to 10 days in advance. Store tightly covered at room temperature.

CHICKEN KABOBS
(Tas Kebap)
Makes 4 servings (pictured on page 18)

2   whole chicken breasts (about 8 ounce each), split, skinned, boned, cut in 2-inch pieces
2   green peppers, cut into 1-inch piece
2   tomatoes, cut into 12 wedges each
¼   cup lemon juice
3   tablespoons butter or margarine, m
1   teaspoon paprika
½   teaspoon salt
¼   teaspoon cayenne pepper

1. Place chicken, green peppers and tomatoes in medium-size bowl. Mix maining ingredients; pour over chic and vegetables. Toss gently to coat. er; let stand at room temperature 1 hour.

2. Heat oven to broil and/or 550°. Thread chicken, green peppers and matoes alternately onto 4 skewers. 4 inches from heat. Turn and baste remaining marinade until chicken i tender, about 20 minutes.